Problems and Strategies of Development in the Eastern Himalaya

Problems and Strategies of Development in the Eastern Himalaya

RANJU R. DHAMALA

GYAN

GYAN PUBLISHING HOUSE

NEW DELHI-110 002

ISBN 81-212-0450-X
Library of Congress Card No. 93-900305

Published in 1993 by
Gyan Publishing House, 5 Ansari Road
New Delhi - 110002

Composed by Refill Master, 162 SBI Ngr, Paschim Vihar, N. Delhi and
Printed at Goyal,Offset Works, Delhi.

CONTENTS

LIST OF CONTRIBUTORS

1. Dr. Rabindra Nath Bhattacharya
   Deptt. of Economics,
   University of North Bengal,
   Distt. Darjeeling.

2. Professor B:K. Roy Burman,
   Centre for the Study of Developing Societies,
   Delhi.

3. Professor Gopal S. Nepali
   Centre for Himalayan Studies,
   University of North Bengal.
   (Currently
   Tribhuvan University
   Kathmandu, Nepal.)

4. Dr. R.K. Kar,
   Deptt. of Anthropology,
   Dibrugarh University,
   Assam.

5. Dr. Dawa Norbu,
   School of International Studies,
   Jawaharlal Nehru University,
   New Delhi.

6. Professor Manas Das Gupta,
   Deptt. of Economics,
   University of North Bengal.

7. Professor B.P. Misra,
Centre for Himalayan Studies,
University of North Bengal.

8. Dr. Saswati Biswas,
Deptt. of Sociology and Social Anthropology,
University of North Bengal.

9. Professor N. C. Choudhury,
Deptt. of Sociology and Social Anthropology,
University of North Bengal.

10. Shri Kanchan Sarkar,
Deptt. of Sociology and Social Anthropology,
University of North Bengal.

11. Dr. P.K. Chakravarty,
Deptt. of Geography and Applied Geography,
University of North Bengal.

12. Dr. Ranju R. Dhamala,
Centre for Himalayan Studies,
University of North Bengal.

EDITOR'S INTRODUCTION

There is a growing acceptance of the fact that problems facing the hill region differ from the plain zone because of its topography and ecological setting. This calls for the formulation of different strategies for the development of these regions. It was with the objective of identifying the problems and suggest measures which will help in the formulation of strategies of development in the Eastern Himalayan region that the Centre for Himalayan Studies, University of North Bengal organised a seminar on the 'Problems and Strategies of Development in the Eastern Himalayan Region'. This volume contains most of the papers presented at the seminar.

'Development and Environment : A Perspective for Hill Region' (Rabindra Nath Bhattacharya) focuses on the concept of sustainable economic development and its relevance to the problem of development and environmental transformation in the Eastern Himalayan region. The sustainable development approach stresses not only the basic need strategy but also that the strategies which are being formulated and implemented should be environmentally sustainable. It entails a dynamic interacting process, whether biological/ecological, economic or social. The author has attempted to formulate an analytical framework by assimilating the ideas advocated by Norgaard, Sachs and Barbier. He proposes that given the diverse ecosystem of the Himalayan region, the sustainable economic development perspective is pertinent to it. This, he has illustrated with the help of some examples from the field of agriculture.

In 'Basic Approach to Planning and Development in North East India' (B.K. Roy Burman) the author underlines the need for the consideration of various contexts of North East India like geo-political, historical-political and historical and social environment while formulating the development strategy for the region. Problems confronting the region are unique. He speaks of demographic paradox and paradox of too much and too little development in terms of statistical parameters. Besides, the region is inhabited by numerous tribes having various indigenous rules of law; communal land holding system and so on. Hence, implementation of any developmental schemes based on an all-India pattern may not produce the desired result, and in some cases, may even become a source of trouble. These necessitate the formulation and implementation of plans at the grass-root level in which the village council shall play significant role. To achieve this, he stresses on the need of undertaking a pilot project in one of the villages of the region to find out the viability of programme, after which it can be tried in few other villages with diverse ethno-social, techno-economic and historical-ecological settings. Only a sustained study of this type, he maintains, will enable us 'to define more sharply the contours of an appropriate strategy of planning and development in this region.'

'Some Sociological Aspects of Development in the Eastern Himalaya' (Gopal S. Nepali) takes up the issue of reconciliation between indigenous culture and the implementation of developmental schemes in the context of hill regions of the Himalayas like Nepal, Bhutan and Sikkim. For him any formulation of development strategy should also consider the ecological and cultural setting and cultural framework of the people for whom the development is intended. Failing to do this, he says, may result in many dysfunctionalities. Nepali substantiates this point by referring to many developmental experiences in Nepal, Bhutan and Sikkim. To prevent any disorganisation and to counter any dysfunctional consequences arising out of development a bunch of innovation may be introduced for the implementation of which the local leaders could play an effective role.

'A Small Tribe in the Eastern Himalaya : An Appraisal of its Problem and Development' (R.K. Kar) tries to present the social framework of the Singhphos of Arunachal Pradesh. He has highlighted the problems confronting the tribe and prescribes various remedial measures which will also help in evolving a strategy of development.

'Changes in Tibetan Economy : 1959-76' (Dawa Norbu) discusses the development of Tibet in the field of industry, agriculture and animal husbandry. It not only provides the official account of the progress achieved in these areas between 1959-76 but also examines it in the light of statements of refugees crossing the Himalaya during the early 60's and 70's and the viewpoints of scholars and journalists who visited Tibet during the period.

From Tibet we shift our attention to Bhutan. It is the least populated country whose economy is traditional with subsistence agriculture and animal husbandry contributing a large part of the gross domestic product. 'Problems of Economic Development in Bhutan' (Manas Dasgupta) focuses on such problems in course of presenting a survey of the main developmental programmes undertaken by the Government Bhutan. The study shows that the priorities in the plans have been development of infrastructure, development of human resources and rural upliftment. However, the fruits of development have failed to percolate to the masses in spite of the 'basic need approach' of the planning process and he attributes this to the adoption of the 'top down approach' which inhibits the participation of the masses and modernisation remains confined to certain areas of production. Bhutan is also dependent on India in respect of financial and technical assistance which has created some problems in the social and economic field. Its desire to overcome these problems is reflected in its policy of diversifying sources of loans and acquiring membership of regional and international organisations.

'Economic Development of Bhutan: Problems and Strategies'

(B.P. Misra) highlights the strategies of plan formulation in Bhutan. It gives the socio-economic condition of Bhutan before the introduction of planned development and the pattern of Indo-Bhutanese relations as these have important bearing on the formulation of the country's plan strategy. The author points out that development in Bhutan has been primarily a political decision because of its desire to ensure its status as an independent monarchical state as also a common perception of problems by both Bhutan and India arising out of Chinese presence and its design in the north. Keeping these points in mind, the emphasis has been on the development of infrastructure, development of human resources and to establish links with foreign countries besides India.

There are three papers on problems and strategies of development in the Darjeeling district. 'Development Strategy in the Hill Areas of Darjeeling : A Critical Appraisal' (Saswati Biswas) presents a critical review of developmental strategy in the hill areas of the District covering a period following the Independence upto the Seventh Plan. Considering the distinct character of the region as compared to other parts of West Bengal in respect of topography and culture, she opines, a different approach should have been adopted, but a study of the plan programmes belies this expectation. There was, of course, acceptance at the governmental level of the need of separate approach to hill development and accordingly the Hill Development Council was set up with this objective but it did not usher in any change. She concludes that the 'quick return approach' of the government relegated the 'long term development perspective' to a background of triviality. The development planners have not as yet laid out a detailed plan for a strategy of development.

'Hill Villages of Darjeeling : Aspects of Economy. Ecology and Agricultural Modernisation' (N.C. Choudhury and Kanchan Sarkar) is based on the finding of a study conducted in ten villages located at different altitudes in Kurseong and Sadar sub-divisions of Darjeeling district. It investigates the immense pressure emanating from an increasing population, ecological degradation and explores some possible ways out through scientific management of agriculture without further disturbing the ecological balance and also by creating employment opportunities through the setting up of small scale industries or encouraging self-employment schemes.

'Problems and Strategies of Development in the Darjeeling Himalaya' (P.K. Chakravorty) identifies the various problems confronting the developmental process in the region, recommends a number of objective and strategy and steps for the implementation of developmental programmes so that the goals of development may be achieved.

'Panchayati Raj Institutions in Sikkim as an Instrument of Development' by this editor is a study on the working of PRIs in Sikkim.

Although the paper focuses on various regions of the eastern Himalaya all the authors have emphasised on the need of grass root participation and the maintenance of ecological balance, both social and biological while formulating the strategies of development.

The primary task of organising this seminar was shouldered by Professor B.P. Misra, former Director who was also the Seminar Director. Without his involvement, the seminar and this volume would not have materialised. It is my privilege that the responsibility of editing was entrusted to me. While organising the papers, I have tried to maintain a thematic and area-wise continuity. However, some inconsistencies in the arrangement of papers in terms of area might have crept in. I hope to be excused for this.

I wish to thank the members of the staff of the Centre for their kind cooperation and secretarial assistance. I acknowledge with thanks the swift and efficient typing done by Shri Jiten Sarkar.

Thanks are also due to Shri B.P. Garg of Gyan Publishing House, New Delhi, for his keen interest in the publication of this volume.

Centre for Himalayan Studies
University of North Bengal
Raja Rammohanpur
Darjeeling, West Bengal

Ranju R. Dhamala

1

Development and Environment—A Perspective for Hill Regions

RABINDRA NATH BHATTACHARYA

Recent years have witnessed a new kind of awareness in development perspective. The new outlook stresses meeting the basic needs of the poor, advocates cultural diversity and recommends 'grassroot' participation in the developmental process. It emphasises that 'real' improvement cannot occur unless the strategies which are being formulated and implemented are environmentally sustainable. As a result, there is a growing 'recognition that the overall goals of environment and development are not in conflict but are indeed the same, namely the improvement of the human quality of life or welfare for present and future generations'.[1] This paper limits itself to discussing the sustainable economic development perspective in a general way and points to the relevance of this perspective to problems of development and environmental transformation in regions like the Eastern Himalayas. Issues having close resemblance to the problems and strategies of development in hill regions have been raised by different scholars as well as by several global organisations. Attempts were made to formalise them in terms of developing some analytical framework. Three of them seems to be more promising. This paper, without being original, attempts to assimilate them in one conceptual framework which may be utilized to identify problems and formulate strategies of development for regions like Eastern Himalaya.

The Perspective of Sustainable Economic Development

While subsuming the 'basic need strategy'[2] the sustainable development approach emphasises that for a 'real' development in Third World countries the strategies which are being formulated and implemented have to be inter-generationally and environmentally sustainable, consistent with social values and institutions (which may not, though, remain static), and have to ensure 'grassroots' participation in the developmental process. The emerging idea of achieving continuous economic and social development along with rational management of environment pre-supposes a re-definition of objectives and methods of action. "The environment is a dimension of development, and must, therefore, be internalized at every decision-making level."[3]

Poor people for their survival are forced to damage environment with long-term consequences (sometimes irreversible). Their livestock over-graze their shortening fallows on steep slopes and fragile soils induce erosion; their need for off-season incomes and fuel drives them to fell and consume/sell fuel wood and to make and sell charcoal; they are forced to cultivate and degrade marginal and unstable land. 'Putting people first, and enabling them to meet their needs, can be then, to reduce these pressures, to reduce degradation, and to maintain potentials for sustainable agriculture and sustainable development at higher levels of productivity. And this, in turn, means that more people in future can have adequate, secure, and decent levels of living.'[4]

It is true that rapid population growth and uneven distribution in some areas complicates natural resource management, it is also undeniable that population pressures on resources usually reflect an extremely skewed distribution of resources. When local inhabitants encroach on forests or cultivate erodible hill side, population pressure is blamed, but the pressure usually stems from the concentration of land-holdings and from the conspicuous absence of meaningful alternative (less resource using) economic activities.

Thus, the basic premise of sustainable economic development is that 'many environmental problems in developing countries originate from lack of development, that is from the struggle to overcome extreme conditions of poverty.'[5] Poor people, in the absence of alternatives, often have to opt for short-run economic gains at the expense of the long-run sustainability of their livelihoods. For instance, one of the consequences of deforestation and the depletion of fuelwood availability is that it compels the poor households to divert dung for use as fuel rather than for fertilizer. It is to be noted that 'the context is one where there is no choice anyway since there are neither fuel nor fertilizer substitutes to which households can gain access.'[6] The result, however, is invariably a decline in soil fertility, low levels of productivity, and loss of future economic welfare.

The primary concern of sustainable economic development is ensuring that the poor have access to sustainable and secure livelihoods. To attain this, national level macro economic approaches are not enough. Ultimately the focus must be on the needs, capabilities, priorities and involvement of the people who are supposed to benefit from them. Otherwise attempts to reduce environmental degradation will be counter-productive. The social forestry programmes in India have failed in the past to have any significant impact on the landless, small and marginal farm households. This was because of a limited commitment to serving community needs, the lack of involvement of poor women (who collect fuel-wood and fodder), and the distrust of social forestry programmes by the landless.[7]

The following criteria then underlie sustainable economic development:[8]

(i) 'Sustainability' pre-supposes total development of society and depends on the interaction of economic changes with social, cultural and ecological transformations;

(ii) Its quantitative dimension (e.g., to increase in food, real income, life expectancy, etc.) is associated with increases in the material means available to those living or destined to live, in absolute poverty, so as to provide for adequate physical and social well-being and security against becoming poorer;

(iii) Its qualitative dimension is multifacet, (e.g. cultural diversity, social cohesion and stability, improvements in environmental quality, greater self-esteem, etc.), and is associated with ensuring the long term ecological, social, and cultural potential for supporting economic activity and structural change.

A Tentative Analytical Framework

Analytical framework to capture the criteria underlying sustainable economic development is yet to develop in full bloom. In what follows, this paper by assimilating the ideas thrown by Norgaard,[9] Sachs[10] and Barbier[11] tries to record some basic steps required in formulating such a framework.

Since sustainable economic development entails a dynamic interacting process, Barbier views this process as an interaction among three systems, the biological (and other resource) system (BS), the economic system (ES), and the social system (SS). Norgaard considers a co-evolutionary interaction of the ecosystem and the socio-system while Sachs looks into three sub-systems within the environment: the natural environment, the man-made techno structures, and the social environment. Barbier's approach captures the other two. In his framework, each system has its own set of human-ascribed goals.

(i) Biological system goals: genetic diversity, resilience, biological productivity.

(ii) Economic system goals: satisfying basic needs (reducing poverty), equity enhancing, increasing useful goods and services;

(iii) Social system goals: cultural diversity, institutional sustainability, social justice, participation.

The general objective of sustainable economic development, then, is to maximize the common elements of the three sets of goals. In contrast, the conventional approach to economic development attempts to maximise only 'ES' goals.

Since over any relevant time horizon it is not possible to maximize these goals all at a time, sustainable development involves a 'process of trade-offs' among the various goals of these three systems. For example, as the economic process of production and consumption is dependent on resource use, increasing even useful goods and services may conflict with ensuring the maximum productivity and genetic diversity of the biological and resource system. The process of trade-offs must also be 'adaptive'. As individual preferences, social norms, economic conditions, etc. change over time, so must be relative weights attached to the various goals.

As economic, social and ecological conditions vary in different location and situations, priorities among goals should also differ. For instance, in the mountainous Himalayas, biological and resource productivity, resilience and genetic and cultural diversity, are clearly a high priority.

The Himalaya and Sustainable Economic Development

The ecosystems of Himalaya from east to west appear in the following order: the tropical rain forest zone, succeeded by the terai foot-hills zone, then horizontally above them in succession, the temperate forests zone, the alpine and tundra zones.'[12] The tropical rain forest zones covers the foothills, lower valleys and flanks of the lesser Himalayan ranges upto a height of 5000 ft. Human habitats are mostly located here. The ecosystem here is the most complex of any found in the Himalaya. It has three important characteristics: (i) the unperturbed natural system has an unusually large number of different species competing for living room in the midst of dense undergrowth, (ii) even with a highly specialised system of nutrient re-cycling the recovery path of the system after a perturbation is not easily predictable and generally show a poor regenerative capacity, and (iii) the real economic productivity is low and uncertain.

Given this ecosystem, we now propose to illustrate, with the help of some examples from the field of agriculture, the relevance of sustainable economic development perspective to areas like Himalaya. This does not, of course, preclude its relevance to other forms of economic and social activities including industry.

Odum[13] characterizes agricultural development as a transformation of the eco-system to reduce number of species and usually lower combined efficiency of nutrient re-cycling, higher but less stable rates of production, and low biomass stocks relative to natural conditions. As man pushes an eco system to suit his own needs, he intervenes in some of the nutrient cycles and disturbs some of the equilibrating mechanisms which has evolved within the natural system. Sustainable development occurs if the social and economic systems compensate for these losses within the natural system. Functions of new social and economic systems might include managing legumes to replace portions of lost nutrient cycles, weeding to offset natural succession, and combating herbivorous insects to compensate for lost natural pest control mechanisms.[14] These new socio-economic functions may entail managerial effort, the acquisition of knowledge, the use of exhaustible natural resources, and modification and support of institutions. Additionally, the socio-economic systems may have to combat an increasing social polarization and more inequitable distribution of income that the whole process may entail (as happened in "green revolution" areas).

Using plain-zone energy-intensive approaches to agriculture in a hilly tropical rain forest entails high transactions costs. The social and economic systems must maintain better roads, storage facilities, and exchange systems for cash crops using produced inputs. More sophisticated credit, risk-sharing, and extension programmes are required to counteract the unpredictable yields of mono cultures of crops unsuited to this biological/ecological system. The necessary layer of businessmen, bureaucrats and technicians on top of an otherwise agrarian society also increases the diversity in education and values and hence, the difficulties of defining and attaining social and economic goals. The resulting high transaction costs (involving trade-offs) are symptoms of the social, economic and biological/ecological mismatch. The consequent process of social degeneration is shared with the environment. Habitat transformation, species extinction, and soil destruction are the likely environmental costs.[15]

The key characteristics of the social and biological/ecological systems in Himalayan tropical rain forests suggest that for sustainable agricultural development an initially compatible social and economic systems would emphasize (1) a multiple product (including perennials), regional, near-subsistence economy, (2) participation of native people with knowledge of the natural system, (3) technologies that evolved in the indegeneous environment, (4) formal and informal risk sharing, and (5) decision-making power in the hands of people close to the dynamic eco system/biological system.

References

1. P. Barletmus : *Environment and Development* (London, Allen & Unwin, 1986), pp. 13-4.

2. P. Streeten : *Development Perspective* (U.K., Macmillan, 1981).

3. I. Sachs : "Alternative Patterns of Development" in *Environment and Development*, ed. by D.M. Dwerkin, (Indiana SCOPE, 1974), p. 386.

4. R. Chambers : *Sustainable Livelihoods : An opportunity for the World Commission on Environment and Development*, (U.K., University of Sussex, Institute of Development Studies, 1986), p. 7. Quoted in E.B. Barbier "The Concept of Sustainable Economic Development" *Environmental Conservation* 14 (2), (1987), pp. 101-110.

5. Barletmus, *op. cit.*, p. 18.

6 D.W. Pearce: *The Sustainable Use of Natural Resources in Developing Countries* Discussion paper 36-15 (London, University College, Deptt. of Economics, (Mimeo), (1986), pp. 5-6. Quoted in Barbier. *Loc. cit.*

7. Centre for Science and Environment : *The State of India's Environment, 1984-85 the Second Citizen's Report* (New Delhi, 1985).

8. Barbier, *op. cit.*, p. 105.

9. R.B. Norgaard: "Coevolutionary Development Potential". *Land Economics* 60 (2), (1984), pp. 160-161.

10. Sachs, *op. cit.*

11. Barbier, *op.cit.*, pp. 101-110.

12. D.M. Kalapes : "Understanding Himalayan Ecology" in *Studies in Himalayan Ecology and Development Strategies*, ed. by T. Singh and J. Kaur (New Delhi, The English Book Store, 1980), p. 12.

13. E.P. Odum : *Fundamentals of Ecology*, 3rd edition, (Tokyo, Toppan Company Ltd., 1971).

14. R.B. Norgaard: "An Evolutionary Critique and Plea for Pluralism", *Journal of Environmental Economics and Management*, (12, 1985), pp. 382-394.

15. Norgaard (1984), *Loc. cit.*

(This is a slightly revised version of the paper presented at the national seminar on 'Problems and strategies of development in the Eastern Himalayas', at the Centre for Himalayan Studies, University of North Bengal, March 18-19, 1988).

2
Basic Approach to Planning and Development in North-East India

B.K. ROY BURMAN

North East India is the meeting point of South Asia, South East Asia and East Asia. Strategic, political, economic and ideological developments in each of these sub-continents have bearing on one or the other part of North East India. With rapid spread of communication network, geopolitical context will become more and more important. Besides many of the ethnic groups in North-East India have their counter-parts in the adjoining countries.

Policy planners in North East India, will require to have awareness and sensitivity about the happenings in the neighbouring countries of the three sub-continents of Asia.

Ethno-Historical Context

Except for the Hindu and Muslim population of Barak Valley, Caste Hindu and Muslim population of Barahmaputra Valley and non-tribal population of Tripura, most of the indigenous ethnic groups of North East India have tradition of migration from East or South East Asia either directly or through stages.

In post-independence period, during all crisis situations one or the other interest-group in India and outside has tried to take up these grey areas of tradition, to weaken national cohesion. The challenge will be accentuated with intensification of developmental activity. All developments imply some dismantling of some of the existing structures. Unless a significant section of the population is imbued with some sense of ideology, the developmental shock may generate even more serious conflagrations in the future, than what have taken place so long.

To meet the challenge some "patriotic" Indian scholars have tried to project spurious "history", sometime with direct encouragement of the administrative bureaucracy. This is self defeating.

Today all nation-states all over the world are facing new challenges in the wake of technological development. In the face of it national unity in North East India cannot be cemented by harping on spurious past, but by emphasising the significance of India, as the vanguard nation against colonialism and as one committed to non-capitalist path of development. There must, however, be consistent and continuous manifestation of these. Ideological dimension must be there in addition to emotional and material dimensions.

Political Historical Context

Except Tripura, all the parts of North East India, were involved in the organised political systems of one or the other part of the rest of India as well as one or the other part of the organised political entities of South East Asia. Even Tripura was not entirely free form outside involvement. It was only during the colonial rule that they were exclusively involved in the Indian situation as subjects of the common rulers. Along with ethno-history their susceptibilities arising out of this fact of history are to be kept in view.

Another unfortunate fact should not be ignored. In the 19th century when the indigenous ethic and political formations tried to resist the British rule, the rest of the country did not actively sympathize with them. Hence, many of them tend to look upon Indian state as a successor of colonial rule in more than temporal sense. It is, therefore, indispensable that developmental strategy must not be merely "welfare oriented" but also oriented to participation of indigeneous corporate groups in a manner as is conducive to inner democratisation of the groups themselves. Besides, from experiences in other parts of the world, the limits of a welfare-state and the contradictions and abuses inherent in it should also be kept in view. The developmental strategies should be built not only keeping in view the history of the past but also the projected history of the future.

Massive expropriation of resources through misinterpretation of political history

In Manipur and Tripura it is claimed that the King was owner of all land in the property sense. Hence it is asserted that with the accession of these princely states to India, all lands other than those on which personal ownership rights can be established are owned by the State of India. Even the Law Research Institute of Gauhati High Court has accepted these claims without further scrutiny. A careful study of the histories of Manipur and Tripura shows that these claims are not based on incontrovertible facts. On the other hand, land policy of virtual expropriation based on such claims tend to stifle the participatory developmental process and rationalise bureaucratic intervention.

Need for meaningful interpretation of "Rule of Law" as a pre-condition for generation of a participatory development strategy in North-East India

There are two approaches to law,—one is legal positivism which considers 'command law' of the political authority as the source of legitimization, the other is legal pluralism which accepts the law in terms of which the people live their lives as the source of legitimization. During the colonial rule, the command law, of the rulers whose philosophical root lay in Roman law, prevailed. Now there is a growing awareness even among a section of the judiciary about the incongruity of the command law orientation in a democratic society. Unfortunately, the initiatives taken by the North East Council for appraisal of the legal systems in the different states, particularly in matters relating to land and land-based resources, have tended to augment the legal positivistic orientation, notwithstanding some advocacy in favour of legal pluralism in dealing with inheritance, succession rights and minor crimes. This will be a source of trouble in the future. Hence it is to be noted that in many countries like U.S.A. Peru etc. where indigeneous population still survive, the judicial decisions of the 19th century based on command law perspective, are being reversed in recent years. Even in an international treaty signed by U.S.A., Canada, U.S.S.R., Sweden in 1976, in respect of the North Sea, the living laws of the indigeneous people have been recognised as a relevant factor. It is not very unlikely that in a decade or so this will be one of the considerations in deciding various issues between India and her neighbours. Some developments in Arunachal in recent decades are to be carefully examined keeping this in view.

Basic issue of triangular relationship of individual, community and state in the matter of land reform

Land reform in India very correctly envisages abolition of

exploitative intermediaries between the state and the individuals.

But in most tribal areas, tribal cultivators derive only a part of their income from cultivation; they also earn substantially through collection of roots, tubers, leaves and other jungle products. They have access to these resources as members of their respective communities. With commercialisation of minor forest products value of non-agricultural goods will go up. Hence if on the analogies of other areas, community as "intermediary" between the state and the individual land-holders is removed, the tribal household will be actually dispossessed of much larger resources, though their rights over small areas of settled agricultural land will be consolidated.

Technological snag in cadastral survey and preparation of record of rights in the hills.

The current practice in some parts of India is to confine cadastral survey to nine degree slope only, because of technical difficulty of accurate survey at a reasonable cost. This has adversely affected the rights of tribal land-holders in those areas. The exact position in North-East India is to be checked.

Problem of environmental management and the role of community

Frequently it is stated that without strict control by the organs of the state, environmental degradation cannot be prevented. But 'Forest and Tribals' Committee set up by the Ministry of Home Affairs has reported that where communities have been allowed to manage their land and forest resources without interference, they have managed the same well. On the other hand, the fact that even the Minister of Environment and Forest has recently deprecated over-enthusiasm for commercial forestry and cash crops, shows that techno-bureaucratic management is not always based on scientific considerations. Appropriate management of environment will require community initiative but technical guidance of the concerned Government department will also be necessary.

Demographic paradox in North-East India and implication for developmental strategy

In 1981 the density of population per sq. km. in North-East India was 109, compared to 221 for India as a whole. It was as low as 8 in Arunachal and as high as 254 in Assam. But as agriculture is the most important source of livelihood for the population in this region, the density should also be considered with reference to the gross cultivated area. It was much higher in North-East India (587). The lowest density per sq. km. of cultivated area in this region was in Arunachal (483) but even this was much higher than the national average.

Given the present state of mobilisation of the productive forces of the region, it is obvious that low density of population is a statistical myth.

A well thought-out population policy, human resources formation policy and corresponding mix of the labour and capital-intensive technology policy will have to be worked out, keeping the demographic paradox in view.

Paradox of too much and too little development outlay in North-East India, in terms of statistical parameters

The sixth plan outlay was Rs. 891/- per capita at the all India level; it was Rs. 4511 per capita in Arunachal. But it was Rs, 148000 (approx) per sq. km. at all India level and only about Rs. 25000 sq. km. in Arunachal. The position in the other states of the region in the matter of per sq. km. investment was slightly better; but even then it was nowhere near the all India average.

The population live in space. The result of the inequitous developmental investment in space can be illustrated with the following figures. Compared to 2.54 km. road length per thousand population at all India level Arunachal has 21.43 km. but compared to 48.90 km. road length per 100 sq. km. at the all India level, Arunachal has only 13.82 km. Again while against the all India average of 1189 persons per hospital-bed, 599 persons per bed in Arunachal compares quite favourably, a very different picture emerges if the area covered per hospital is considered. It is 497 sq. km. at the all India level and 3798 sq. km. in Arunachal.

It is obvious that the development indicators will have to be suitably modified, to reflect the realities of the region and planning strategy will have to be adjusted accordingly.

Over-emphasis on premature commercialisation and creation of over-dependence in the satisfaction of minimum needs

Land-man ratio in most areas of North-East India is such that by reorienting production schedule many of the basic needs can be satisfied locally. If after ensuring that, massive commercialisation is attempted, the population will be less vulnerable to market manipulation by speculators and monopoly concerns. But in many areas an opposite strategy has been adopted and development outlay has been planned accordingly. Thus, not infrequently, 'development' is suspected to have provided alibi for siphoning off resources from the region.

Performance assessment by spending capacity and creation of neo-feudal rights

The National Committee on Development of Backward Areas has recommended individualisation of communal ownership in the North East for the sake of "progress". As a result, attempts are made to implement development programmes by short-circuiting the community. But only powerful individuals within the community can do it with the support of bureaucracy. This is creating neo-feudal rights where such rights do not exist or exist only in incipient form. In terms of political economy what is taking place is anti-development through "development".

Artificial nature of poverty alleviation programme based on all India norm

Income criterion of determination of poverty on an all India basis is meaningful only if there is a fair degree of uniformity in respect of social infra-structure and culturally determined distributive mechanism. But most of the tribal areas of the country and of the North-East particularly stand on a different footing in these matters. Poverty alleviation in these areas should be two pronged; first, financial investment is to be community based as has been tried, in a halting manner although, in Nagaland. Second, ideological and political investment is to be aimed at internal democratisation of the community, as has been attempted in Tripura. But these two should go together. In Meghalaya, occasional attempts have been made to make a patchwork of the two, but no systematic and well thought-out strategy has been built up to overcome the inevitable internal contradictions that one faces in any such attempt. In Mizoram, a right move in the early 50's was hijacked by political opportunism at all levels, resulting in disastrous consequences. In Arunachal, the story is that of paternalistic ad-hocism; any authentic effort from the grass-root level is yet to come up.

Problem of computability of schemes meant for the poor with their socio-cultural specificities

Analysis of many of the IRDP schemes indicates that their bankability criteria are remarked by urban middle class bias. These are not related to the time budgeting, social organisation of labour, management experience, communication net-work, decision making process, consumption norms and aspiration motivation patterns of the tribal households.

Problems of balanced operation of various sources of institutional finance

With the spread of rural banking and public distribution system through fair price shops, the role of LAMP, as originally envisaged has become largely redundant. On the other hand, there is a need of strengthening local entrepreneurs through primary cooperatives, with minimum official interference. Current policy ambiguities in regard to LAMP and PAC should be removed.

Need to utilise the provision of Agricultural Land Development Loan Act 1883 for waste - land development

This Act provides for group loan whose repayment can be stretched to 35 years by relating the same to the phase of generation of productive capacity and also by indicating individual responsibility subsumed within the group context. There is a possibility that the provisions of this Act might have been misused by feudal interests in the plains in the past. But in the tribal context of North East, with its egalitarian ethos and growing democratic assertion this Act seems to be most suitable for wasteland development with the involvement of community institutions in that region.

Ancillary legislation needed for the community organisations to function as channels for the flow of institutional finance

In Nagaland V.D.B. can attract bank loan. The panchayats in Tripura are also similarly authorised though they do not appear to have taken advantages of it till now. However, the village councils that the recently constituted District Council may set up, should also be similarly authorised. The Autonomous District Councils functioning under the provision of the sixth schedule in the different states of North East should also be authorised to operate bank loan. Greater integration of regulatory and development functions of these bodies set up under the provisions of the constitution is needed.

Role of North-East Council

NEC is functioning primarily as an inter-governmental forum. Perhaps it could play very important role as a bridge organisation between the people and the states. This would require massive investment of NEC in creating communication net-work including the academics, the voluntary organisations, the traditional tribal organisations, the governmental agencies and so on. Frequently in the decision making forum set up by NEC, only the representative of the states and the centres are involved. These require to be much more broad-based.

Role of voluntary agencies

A number of voluntary agencies are operating in North-East India. Either they confine themselves to welfare activities or they combine some philanthropic religious cultural practices with welfarism. These can hardly cope with the ferments taking place in the minds of the younger generation. In this context, the recent trends of "liberation theology" which is taking shape particularly among the Catholics on a global plane is of particular relevance. Sometimes the manifestations of this appear to be anti-Indian but the younger generation of the tribals do not feel convinced. On the other hand indigeneous ideological framework is not coming up in an authentic manner to satisfy the intellectual-moral need of the youth. As a result, voluntary organisations have not been able to strike root in the tribal areas of the region.

Politics of pragmatism, welfarism and at best petty populism that the various national parties are playing in the region, has created vacuum.

Role of the universities and other centres of higher learning

The universities and other centres of higher learning are more serving as conveyors of academically respectable information than as creator of knowledge. Until recently the history of the region was the history provided by the apologists of colonial rule. Only recently a faint quest for an authentic history is perceptible among some historians. But sometimes the alternative interpretative frame tends to become rationalisation of feudal claims. Many anthropologists have attempted to change the images of their discipline as handmaid of colonial establishment. economists in their turn tend to display instant scholarship by fitting facts into 'models' derived from experiences elsewhere. These look impressive but these create mere phantoms of knowledge.

Ethno-philosophy, ethno-epistemology rooted in the soil are not yet respectable. Several inane attempts made in these fields have failed to make any impact.

Bio-physical sciences have by and large remained unconcerned about the society. In the field of Botany, while a big push is given to the study of herbal medicine and of the use-value of plants, but for one or two exceptions, hardly any sustained study has been made on the growth cycles of plant communities. While study of herbal medicine and use-value of plants in isolation would augment commercial exploitation of the same, it is only through the study of growth cycles of plant communities that the mutually adaptive processes of human communities and plant communities can be adequately understood. A rapid review of researches in physics, chemistry, earth and life sciences in one university revealed that hardly any research has been done, which would help in interpreting the quality of life of the population.

If the right priority in scientific researches is lacking, one cannot but feel that the priority is derived from the market value of science and not from the need value of man.

Recapitulation and supplementary observation

What has been attempted in this review is a critique of several stated and unstated assumptions which underline the planning and development strategy in respect of North-East India. Broadly they are as follows:

(i) North-East India being integral part of the organised state power of India, the tribal people are expected to spontaneously involve themselves in the political and socio-cultural processes in India in a positive manner.

(ii) Improvement of the standard of living will by itself enhance the integrative process of the region with the rest of the country.

(iii) The tribal people being backward the burden of developing them will have to be borne by administrative and technical bureaucracy of the state and / or selected voluntary organisations which are frequently rooted in a different milieu.

(iv) Massive investment for commercialisation of the vast resources of the region through a network of institutions manned by administrative and technical bureaucracy will improve the living condition and quality of life of population.

(v) Communal system of access to / control, management and ownership of resources is an impediment to the optimum utilisation of the resources and to the participation of the population in productive enterprises and related economic activities in an effective manner.

(vi) Continuation of communal access to resources will

lead to environmental degradation.

(vii) In the context of growing stratification within tribal societies communal system would mean perpetuation of exploitation of weaker section of the tribals by their own elite section.

(viii) Communal system will ossify the social distance between the concerned tribal communities and others.

(ix) Pursuit of science and technology deriving priorities from the establishments of science and technology, without reference to the social milieu will by itself generate a scientific temper and satisfy the intellectual and spiritual needs of the new generations.

It is not necessary to repeat the arguments for rejection of these assumptions or cardinal principles. To avoid confusion, one or two points will however be briefly touched upon. First, it must be accepted that the tribals of North-East India have as much right of dissidence as any other population in any part of India. The political and socio-cultural processes of India should be as much influenced by them as by any other population of the country. Second, the ranking systems within the tribal communities should not be confused with stratification systems. Third, class implies not only property relation but also structure of consciousness within tribal communities. Those who speak of class contradictions within tribal communities have rarely tried to analyse the totality of their internal and external relations and link up their structure of consciousness with the same.

As regards role of communal resource holding system, it is to be noted that among the Maoris of New Zealand it has been found to provide the basis for large scale capitalist enterprises. Some of the Latin American countries also provide example, on the same line. On the other hand, in U.S.S.R. communal system was used in some parts for socialist transformation by organising clan Soviets.

It is wrong to consider communal land holding system as

representing a particular type or stage of political economy. It represents a form of organisation where role of bureaucracy is minimal and in which there is a conscious interlacing of the ethos of mutuality and of enforced obligations in varying degrees. It follows from this that the pattern of relation of the community and the larger society does not automatically take a particular form simply because of the existence of communal land holding system. Various patterns of internal and external relations are the outcome of various operational strategies.

Need for action research about the viability of communal land holding system

Various organisational forms and organising ideologies are associated with communal land system. For instance, in Manipur the Naga ideology is that of exercise of control by elected representatives of clans supplemented by specific role in management by specific categories of persons. The Kuki ideology is that of control by hereditary chiefs and kin-group elders who enjoy certain prerogatives of office, but who must ensure a minimum fair-share of resources for all members of the community. In Kuki area bureaucratic intervention is promoting neo-feudal tendencies. In Naga area it is creating internal dissentions. Action research may first start in a village with sizeable resource in a Naga area. The traditional village council can be encouraged to set up a body which can be considered as a "legal person". A sizeable area of the community land and forest can be placed at the disposal of the body but the body will be responsible to draw up development plan for the entire resources of the village, including the resources held by individual households. After the development plan has been approved by the village council and confirmed in a meeting of the entire village population, the body would initiate move to obtain development loan of three types (a) Agricultural Land Development loan under the Act of 1883 for reclamation of community land, (b) Crop-loan from cooperative, (c) Term loan from commercial bank for horticulture, forestry etc. as well as for

R and D. Keeping in view the fact that the economy is partly monetised and partly non-monetised in different degrees in different parts of North-East India, re-payment of these loans will also take different forms. Crop loan will be repaid by individuals in cash or kind; loan under the 1883 Act will be repaid partly in cash/ and partly in the form of maintenance of production infra-structure (i.e. road, irrigation channel) by the community. Term loan to individuals will be repaid in cash; term loan for community production will be repaid by the community in the form of creation and maintenance of social infra-structure and rendering some of the social services, which otherwise the state is to render to the community. The incremental income will be distributed among the members of the community according to their traditional and adaptive norms of fair-share upto an agreed ceiling; the rest will be used for building up reserve fund and for repaying loan in kind and services as indicated. Depending on the scale of operation and the output, the social and production infra-structure may have to be shared with the population of the state even outside the resource holding community. Economic value of all the social and production infra-structure created and services rendered to the community (local and supra-local) will be computed and that amount will be paid by the state to the commercial institutions as repayment of loan.

The village level body of the land-holding community will be responsible for decision about policy and operational matters. But appropriate management and technical personnel will be placed at the disposal of the body by the state. They will be on deputation with the village level body and will be paid out of the fund of that body. Thus normal operational efficiency will be ensured without disturbing the autonomy of the body. The state, however, will have the right to give guidance about resource planning and of continuous monitoring of the implementation.

It is obvious that this novel approach will require experimentation about organisation forms and procedural norms for quite some time. One organisational form may be to create an Integrated Resource and Community Development Authority with participation of the representatives of states' universities, tribal population, action-researchers, financial institutions and others. At the initial stage,the fund may be made available partly by NEC and partly by financial institutions through a suitable combination of subsidy and loan.

After the pilot project has made some progress in one village, for the purpose of experimentation and comparison it can be tried in a few other villages with diverse ethno-social, techno-economic and historico-ecological settings. This action research will aim at generating not only commodity, social and production infra-structure and social service output, but also to reinforce the values of reciprocity, equity, and participation, science rooted in social living and wider human commitment.

It is hoped that through sustained and patient action research of the type indicated, it will be possible to define more sharply the contours of an appropriate strategy of planning and development in North-East India.

3

Some Sociological Aspects of Development in the Eastern Himalaya

GOPAL S. NEPALI

Development is a type of social change which is caused by the conscious efforts of man to improve his material, social, cultural and spiritual life. Implicit in its philosophy is the belief that human happiness can be maximised by the greater and greater control of the material environment in the service of man. This is a concept based on the materialistic—mechanistic philosophy bound of the West, which has immensely progressed due to enormous development of science and technology. This philosophy is the natural outcome of the historical development of the Western society and is well integrated into it. This is now being accepted by the non-western world in order to improve the conditions of its people in whose societies the material, social and the spiritual are well integrated and the spiritual is a living part. In these societies the economic part of the society interacts with the non-economic part mutually reinforcing one another. Thus to separate the economic part and to look at it from the western material point of view creates more problems than it can solve.

Another important feature of development concept is that it has a national framework. It is again a western contribution. No items of development, however laudable it may seem as regards the interests of a group for whom it is meant, can be approved and implemented by a central authority if it goes contrary to the overall national interest. A third feature of it is that it is defined, conceived and implemented by a central authority which determines the priorities as well as areas and strategies of development no matter how the people for whom the developmental programme is meant feel about their needs. All these have complicated the problems of development in the third world.

The major efforts in the programme of development has been in the direction of economic development which is to be assisted and supplemented by the introduction of such changes in the non-economic sectors of social organisation as to bring them more in line with modernity. But societies are not dead things. It reacts and refuses to be interfered with indiscriminately. It has its own nature, which has to be understood if we want any modification in its material and non-material parts. One instance of such continued resistance by the traditional feature is the circumvention of the Indian democratic process by caste, especially in the rural areas. Despite our total commitment to the abolition of caste from our society, it is as pervasive as before in many areas and further, it has also crept into new areas of our life.

Both ecological and social framework will determine how a particular item of development will be useful or accepted in a community. There are examples from cross cultural scenes to support this contention. To quote an example from the tribal world, according to the late Prof. Guha, the improvement in the house structure of the Andamanese led to an increase of diseases among them. Likewise Dr. Mazumdar points out that the introduction of the value of civilisation into the tribal societies has resulted into the cultural disorganisation of the tribal people of India leading to the incidence of crime, gambling, prostitution diseases and disappearance of tribal institution which shaped their personality. These instances can be multiplied without number to show that the changes introduced from outside do not always produce the desired results; while on the contrary, they lead to such unintended consequences that may create more miseries for the community than they were intended to remove.

It is also fairly clear, on the basis of several studies, that a community is selective in the acceptance of an alien innovation or culture trait. For example, the Newars of Nepal, who have very high degree of material culture and who have excelled in technological skill, craftsmanship in metalwork and who are traditionally known also for their skill in agriculture have totally refused to this day to use the plough. They stick to their digging hoe, although a plough is an advanced technology as compared to the digging hoe. Side by side, the Gorkhas (Chhetri caste) would be using the plough in their fields located adjacent to the fields of the Newars. It cannot be said that the Newars are ignorant of the plough since they are excellent craftsmen. The fact is if a Newar takes to the plough, he is ex-communicated by their society. But the Newars have willingly accepted the hand tractors which have been introduced from Japan. This serves to show that if any culture item is negatively defined in a community it is not accepted, however, economically it may be beneficial to the community. Social structure exerts its own pressure on whether to accept or not to accept an innovation from outside.

Another example to show the selective nature of a community in matters of accepting an alien culture is again drawn from Nepal. The Government of Nepal has a scheme of inducing the Newar peasants who are widely accepted as skilled cultivators to settle in the terai region. They were offered all kinds of help by the Government. The scheme could not succeed as the Newar peasant caste was reluctant to leave their traditional home in hills, whereas the Chhetri and others took advantage of the opportunity and migrated in good number to the terai to cultivate the newly acquired land after clearing the forests. The refusal of the Newar peasant caste to settle down in the terai is a function of their social organisation. The kinship organisation, especially of the Newar peasant caste is so well knit and the individual and the family in domestic ceremonies are so dependent on it from birth to death that unless the entire kinship group migrates together, social living becomes miserable for a man. For example, in all ceremonies relating to the individual, especially when a death occurs, the role of the married daughters of the house is unavoidable. So a Newar peasant cannot get the continued fulfilling of roles by his kin members in relation to him if he is quite far away.

To conclude, with regard to acceptance or non acceptance of a culture trait, it is necessary, for a planner or his agents to know under what social circumstances what kind of an alien culture or innovation will be accepted by the people for whom the development scheme is to be introduced, since the planned development scheme is another name for bringing about contact between traditional culture and the scientific technological culture.

It is, therefore, necessary to understand the nature of culture. The sociological-anthropological approach regards culture as an integrated whole in which the parts do not make up to an aggregate. They are inter-related and inter-dependent to form a functional system, and the change in one part is reacted upon the other parts and *vice versa*. It is because of this integration that the existence and continuity of society is sustained. Whenever the basic existence and continuity is threatened, the cultural system reacts and develops defence mechanism. It is this view that can explain why an innovation — be it a value of norm, a behaviour pattern or a material item is not accepted by a community, however, rational and beneficial it might appear to them.

But to say that culture is an integrated whole is not to say that its various parts are in perfect harmony. There are so many stresses and strains resulting in some change in some parts or in some elements. But the tendency is towards reaching harmony which, however, never happens in the perfect sense of the term. There are internal causes of such a change, such as, changes in the demographic feature of the population, innovation within the community, imperfect copying across generations, as well as between individuals with regard to their social behaviour pattern, natural calamity, clashes of class and group based interests, as Firth has pointed out. These are auto genetic changes. Given relatively an isolated community, the imbalance created in the functional system of culture is manageable since the adaptive changes take place in the other parts of the system.

The other factor of change is external arising from conquest or contact with an alien culture. Here the situation is different. The impact of the forces of change is quick, continuous and pervasive. This is likely to disturb the internal balance. The status and role of the individuals may get confused leading to a disorganisation of the society.

In view of the above, problems of development of the Himalayan region may be better understood if we look at them from such angle. The communities and tribes that live over these regions are more or less independent culture wholes with the exception of the Nepalis who have developed caste system. These communities and tribes have been living somewhat in isolation from the mainstream of the Indian civilisation on the one hand and on the other also from one another, especially because of the difficult terrain and due to the absence of modern means of communication.

These communities and tribes are almost autonomous in their cultural life and are largely dependent on their natural environment for eking out their livelihood. With the exception of Darjeeling hills, the density of population is small and as we move higher and higher up the hills from the south to the north it becomes still smaller. Thus the density of population of Sikkim is 45, in Bhutan 24 in Arunachal Pradesh 6 while in the Darjeeling hills 214 (Census 1971). Such small populations whose concentrations are confined to certain areas only, can hardly be amenable to modern development and to the kind of distribution of skills needed for the supply of manpower.

Another important feature which should not escape our eyes is the fact that from the ethnic point of view these people are divided into a number of linguistic and cult re-groups of endogamous nature, and separated from others not only by geographical isolation but also by rigidity of cultural traditions as is reflected in their respective social organisations. Broadly speaking, they occupy different altitudinal zones ranging between the alpine zone on the north and the tropical foothills in the terai. The higher mountainous regions are occupied by the Tibetans and Tibetan-like people who either do dry farming or combine it with pastoral economy and trade with Tibet. The people of the middle zone i.e. who live on the lower hills and in the mountainous valleys belong to Hindu communities or semi-Hinduised groups of Mongoloid origin. They live on irrigative cultivation, trade and animal husbandry and the people who live on the tropical or sub tropical regions also live on wet cultivation and trade of domestic type. A basic feature of the entire region has been that the majority of the people depend on agriculture and forest products. Because of the comparative absence of roads, the marketability of the produce cannot find any easy outlet. At the same time the domestic market is very much limited because of small populations and low purchasing powers of the local people.

The environment of the hills has also imposed its constraints on the people to which the communities have adjusted. Thus each culture group along with its social organisation has adapted itself to the environment, which, when looked at from the point of view of the main stream culture of India is a life of hard misery and material and economic poverty. The predominance of spiritual and magical institutions as in the case of the people of Sikkim, Bhutan and Arunachal, is an anathema to the scientific technological oriented planners of the country. And here lies the rub. To the people these beliefs and practices play very important role in their social, political and economic life. How to meet these spiritual bases of their society introducing modern technology and rationality without doing damage to their existence is a fundamental issue. The property system, clan system, lineage system and economic system are all intertwined and interdependent with the religious system. So to replace their traditional economic institutions with modern economic institutions would mean the very undermining of the existence of the social organisation of these hill people.

How developmental attempts lead to the imbalance in the local society can be found in the case of Sikkim. The Nepalese ethnic groups being hard working and skillful workers and cultivators were imported into Sikkim to develop agriculture and trade of the country. Nepalese labour has been essential for the progress of Sikkim. But the cost is also not too little. Because of high fertility among the Nepalese and their continued migration, the Bhutia Lepcha population is on the way of being extinct and Nepalese culture has supplanted the Bhutia Lepcha culture. The Nepalese institutions of marriage, Nepali language and demographic superiority over the Tibetan acculturated people have led to this state of affairs in the region, both through the rapid rise of the Nepalese population and sanskritisation of the Lepchas who live inter-mixed with the Nepalese in the southern part of the country. The political and economic integration of Sikkim into the Indian republic has been entirely due to the Nepalese ethnic groups as a majority community who voted for the merger of that country. Development creates such unintended consequences which have to be foreseen in the beginning.

In Bhutan also the population dynamics of the Bhotias, the Nepalese and the people of Indian origin may in the long run, result in favour of the numerical superiority of the Nepalese ethnic groups. Although sociological data with regard to Bhutan are meagre due to the state policy, it is guessed that Bhutan has a sizeable population of the Nepalese ethnic groups, say about 30 to 40 per cent. They have settled down in the south western part of the country. As the Nepalese are said to be very efficient labour and have the physiological capacity to quickly adapt themselves to different kinds of climatic and environmental conditions, they have a tendency to displace or assimilate the Tibeto-Burman tribes. Wherever they have gone, this has happened. Their marriage and family organisations provide a lot of freedom to the individuals to take wives from the other communities, in addition to one from one's own caste. Being a patrilineal community, the children born out of such mixed wedlocks are affiliated to the father's group. Besides, the fertility of the Nepalese women have been found to be greater than the Tibeto-Burman community or tribes as the studies from other region show. From the point of view of marriage ideology, the Nepalese have been polygynous whereas the Tibeto-Burman tribes of Tibetan acculturation have been polyandrous. This single factor had in the past helped the Nepalese to multiply their population so fast that today in the Himalayan region as a whole from western Nepal to Sikkim their population is overwhelming.

Besides, their non-rigidity in matters of inter-mixing and establishing connubial relations,as well as bending their brand of Hinduism to accommodate the non-Hindu tribes of the Himalayas through the mechanism of Nepali Brahmin, has enabled these Nepalese to add to their group through the sanskritisation of these Mongoloid groups. This is the process by which the Tibeto-Burman tribes such as the Magar, Gurung, Limbu, Rai, Tamang, Sherpa, a part of the Lepchas and some others have been affiliated to the Nepalese ethnic groups. In fact, the Nepalese have played a very significant role in the Indianization of the Himalayas through the affiliation of these Tibeto-Burman tribes into Nepalese ethnic groups.

Bhutan as a developing nation has got to modernise itself if it is not be continued to be called a backward country. Its industrialisation and modernisation, besides for its own prosperity, is a function of world pressure. The need for greater pace of development will require a massive amount of skilled manpower to man the different sectors of country's trade, economy and administration. Such a massive supply of skilled power is beyond the capacity of Bhotiya population, especially because of country's religio-social-political system. The identity of the Bhutanese culture and society is co-terminous with the existence of monastic institutions and their predominant importance in the overall society.

But the existence and continuity of the monastic institutions, and thereby of the Bhutanese cannot be possible with the demand for the skilled manpower to match the needed pace of development. It must make a grim choice either to cut back the pace of development or draw upon the Nepalese and the people of Indian origin for the supply of skilled man power. In the long run, the inter-regional migration, which, as a matter of ethnic policy, is not permitted, may have to go if Bhutan is to desire for the elimination of regional imbalances in its development. The greater part of the country especially in the higher hills, development has very negligible appearance. But economic rationality will force Bhutan to make equitable distribution of its resources to exploit the wealth of its natural environment. Even for the scientific development of agriculture and animal husbandry in the upper region, the Nepalese skilled labour force will be economically a necessity, as the people of Indian origin will not be ethnically predisposed to migrate to the higher regions on the climatic ground. Thus the rising population of the Nepalese as efficient labour force to migrate to the other places where today they are not allowed is likely to change the ethnic dynamics of the country in the long run.

To a certain extent, the Bhutanese manpower for meeting the requirement of development could be augmented by effecting some modification in the recruitment of monks and nuns to divert some of them to developmental purpose. Bhutan can follow the example of Thailand where there is the practice of initating the males and females into monkhood and nunnery for some fixed period, after which the initiates can come back to join their families as laymen. But it is differential birthrate quality which will ultimately decide the ethnic dynamics of the country if we assume that greater care of health are equally available to all the communities making the death rate uniform and that the migration from Tibet is negligible.

Therefore, the problem of development in the hill region of the Himalayas is one of preserving the indigenous culture and society while at the same time ensuring the material social development of the region to enable the people to partake in the fruits of the achievement of India as an industrialised nation.

Another anthropological concept which we can apply with profit for development in the Himalayas is the concept of sub-cultural world. In the Eastern Himalayas as a whole, we may take each of the ethnic groups and the tribes as an organic whole. Because of the effective functioning of each of the ethnic groups and tribes as a separate sub-cultural world the personality development of the individuals in each of these groups may not be identical. The capacity of learning, the attitude towards change and the eagerness to accept a particular innovation may vary as between the people of the sub-cultural worlds. This is of vital importance when we introduce a change. We must have development plans like micro-hydro power schemes which can be managed by a group of families or clans.

The concept of sub-cultural world may be useful still in another way especially, among the Nepalese among whom caste is the basis for dividing people into hierarchic groups based on ritual consideration. If an innovation is introduced at the higher point on the social ladder, the chances of its acceptance by the community may be enhanced as it becomes the prestigious value of higher group and thereby becoming an object of imitation, under the process of sanskritisation, by the lower castes.

Another important concept is the differentiation between form, function and meaning. Every culture trait has a form, function and meaning. An item of culture or innovation may not be identically perceived by the individuals of different culture groups. Barnett has pointed out that the form which is the overt expression of a trait, appears to take precedence over other two qualities as determinant of change. If the form is differently perceived in the value system of two different cultures,it will be differently accepted by the prospective recipients. But if the form can be reinterpreted to conform to the patterns of meaning of the recipient culture and retain essentially its original functions, it may be accepted. Only on this basis can we explain the reinterpretation of the aboriginal gods as higher gods of the Hindus. Such syncratic process has become very handy in the spread of Christianity in Africa among the tribes. Thus an innovation may be acceptable to the culture groups of the hills—be it a caste or a tribe–if it can be reinterpreted to conform to their own value system. This is the technique we may employ to overcome the traditional resistance to change in the Himalayas.

Again, inter-ethnic conflict or inter-village conflict is another dimension of the life of the hill people. These conflicts may be reinforced and supported through mythology, assumed historical events and village festivals and rituals resulting in the overt expression of it in the day-to-day life of the inhabitants of a region. Such sentiments of conflict could be manipulated to the advantage of the developmental purpose. Thus the sociological significance of the various structural level of co-operation and conflict is important as these reveal the reality of the local social structure.

Given the range of change permissible by the structural functioning of a group or society, the success of the developmental efforts depends on the leadership tapped to influence the people to adopt the change. Here again, the sub-cultural training of the administrative personnel, their moral status in the recipient community and their image in the total traditional social hierarchy could do much to influence the people. In the hill areas, the traditional leaders still control the decision making process of the local society.

Any lack of cooperation between the administrator and the local leadership may create mistrust and conflict. For example, concepts like 'environment' and 'ecology' do not evoke the same reaction as felt by the Government and the aid missions. Forestation and taking care of the resources do not belong to the 'dharma' of the peasant, It is the 'Raj Dharma'. Hence the spread of new ideas and the implementation of the programme largely devolves on the active cooperation of the local village or clan leadership. A study from Nepal shows that among the Tibeto-Burman tribes, the traditional leaders still control the masses and in matters of the solutions and interpretation of the crisis situations, they still follow their traditional leaders blindly. In the places where the hold of the magico-religious leaders is still strong, a development strategy that is neglectful of these leaders will have negative impact on the authority of these leaders. And this is surely not likely to evoke the generation of local support. The strategy should be to assimilate such local leadership into the development efforts to bring successful results.

To sum up, the Himalayan communities and tribes should be regarded as organic wholes which have different cultural and mental capacities to absorb the ideas, behaviour pattern, institutions and material and social skills brought from outside as items of development. Secondly, the introduction of developmental inputs must take account of the internal imbalances that may be created as a consequence, in as much as the traditional fit between the religious, the social, the political, the economic and the environmental gets disturbed without having achieved a new fit. To prevent disorganisation as in the case of the tribals of the plains of India, some positive steps by way of inter-related bunch of innovations may be introduced to counteract the disfunctional consequences arising out of the developmental efforts. Each tribe or ethnic group and its mental and social ability should be borne in mind while implementing the developmental programmes. And finally, the local leadership and the traditional technology may be of immense help both for their further improvement and for an effective use to manage the specific programmes that yield immediate benefits to the local population.

4

A Small Tribe in the Eastern Himalaya: An Appraisal of its Problems and Development

R.K. KAR

The strategy of development of any area or community requires defining in clear terms the contents of development. Development is a value-loaded term, as it signifies a process of change in the desired direction. It is an invisible whole, although for the sake of convenience it is divided into economic, political, cultural, educational, spiritual and the like. It is a harmonious, balanced progress in different spheres of individual and societal life. Lop-sided progress in one sphere is often at the expenses of progress in another (others). When this happens, over-all development, which we want to maximize, becomes a causality. Understanding of the framework of social structure and social organisation of any group is, therefore, essential before contemplating some plan of action to bring some changes in the community.

In the social life of the Himalayan communities though certain common characteristics cut across the geographical regions, yet, there are some strong local variations. The nature of the terrain is one of the important factors that form the matrix of social life. All societies depend on it for their basic needs. Social history, ethnic composition and social environment are some of the other important factors. All these embody some concept of a functional kind that may, however, be relativistic in nature. Thus, for example, people, not accustomed to the practice of bride price may find it difficult to realise that the system does not mean selling of bride for an agreed upon price, but has, on the contrary, some wider social implications.[1] Being accustomed to the idea of monogamy, we may criticise some of the groups on the score of polygamy. We hardly realise that there is an economic reason for it. The regions where it prevails have very little cultivable land. The Kinnaurs and the people of Jaunsar-Bawar, the Lahaulis, Spitians and Todas who practice it, have to keep down the population. This reason may not sound adequate to many of us, but it is a fact that the system has not been prompted by any prejudice against womanhood. "Women are nowhere so free as in these parts of India, whether for marriage or divorce or freedom on movement and occupation[2]".

Each community has certain distinctive characteristic rooted in the remote past which bear the impress of that culture. As regards the role of specific beliefs and pratices in determining the response of the community to specific items of development programme, Roy Burman[3] reports" .... though commodious houses had been constructed by the Government for the tribal Rabhas, they continued to live in their traditional type of huts without light and ventilation, they agreed to keep only their cattle and poultry birds in the improved huts. The Rabhas explained that their ancestral spirits would not agree to live in the new type of huts and they cannot shift there abandoning the ancestral spirits. Here, the housing programme, executed without taking into consideration the cultural tradition of the community proved a failure".

Sometimes an arbitrary or generic term is used to denote a group of tribes living in a certain territory. All the tribes occupying the same geographic region are called by outsiders by the same common term. It is a common feature in the north-eastern Himalayan region. For example, the expression 'Naga' is a common term to denote the people from Nagaland, but the group of the Nagas includes in itself, tribes like Angami, Ao, Chakhesang, Chang, Khienmungan, Konyak, Lhota, Phom, Rengma, Sangtam, Sema, Yimchung and Zeliang. Similarly, the Kukis of Manipur, the Adis of Arunachal Pradesh, the Paharis of Rajmahal hills, the Gadabas of Orissa and the Gonds of western India are not homogenous population in respect of ethnicity, language, social history and tradition.[4]

A good deal of insight in social dimension is, therefore, necessary for the formulation of right strategy for the development of any community.

Keeping these facts in mind, the paper attempts an appraisal of the socio-political life of the Singphos, a small tribe in Arunachal Pradesh in the eastern Himalayas, it also attempts to identify some of the problems confronted by the people that needs attention on priority basis.

The paper is based on the secondary sources as well as on field work. Field trips were undertaken in the Bordumsa area in 1973 and in 1984.

The Land and the People

Arunachal Pradesh is a mountainous tract covering area of 83,578 sq. km., in the eastern Himalaya. The land is bounded by Bhutan in the west, Tibet and China in the North-East and Assam in the south. It consists of sub-montane and mountainous ranges sloping to the plains of Assam.

According to the 1981 Census, the total population of the territory is 628,050. The density is 7 per sq. km. as against the all-

India figure of 211. The male-female ratio in Arunachal Pradesh is 100 : 90 whereas the all-India figure is 100 : 93.5. Total tribal population in territory is 441,000 (69.82%). The percentage of literacy is 20.09 as against the all-India figure 36.17.[5]

In this land of picturesque beauty live a number of tribes and sub-tribes possessing a rich variety of cultures and folklores. There are as many as 25 major tribal groups which can further be divided into 80 or more sub-groups.[6] Some of the widely known groups are as follows : Adi, Aka, Apatani, Bangni, Hill Miri, Khamba, Khampti, Khowa, Memba, Miji, Monpa, Nishi, (Dafla), Nocte, Sherdukpen, Singpho, Sulung, Tagin, Tangsa, Wancho and Yobin.

These groups are divided and sub-divided into numerous sub-groups and clans, each with some distinctive features. For example, the Adi has 18 known sub-divisions, the Tangsa has 31 distinct sub-groups and the Bangni has 4 such divisions. There are some 25 other small groups which do not belong to any of the larger groups, and have their distinct cultures.[7] Names of 110 tribes were returned in 1971 census in Arunachal Pradesh.

Racially, the people are predominantly of Mongoloid stock. But notable inter-group variations exist among them in many spheres of life, their settlement pattern, language/dialect, nature of local, government, economic pursuit, religion, etc.

The people live in villages, though each tribe has different patterns of village settlement. There are long-established Nocte and Monpa villages, the Nishis and Tagins have frequently shifting settlements, whereas among the Nishis and Mishmis, villages may consist of only one or two houses, which are, often, very large where 60 or 70 persons reside. Generally, the hill villages consists of 200 to 500 inhabitants. Many of these villages are pleasantly located on hill tops with wonderful views of rivers, forests and mountains.

The mother-tongue data collected by the Census department reveals that there are about 170 indigenous and non-indigenous dialect/language in the territory. The most frequently used non-indigenous language is Nepali. Others with reasonable frequency are Hindi, Assamese and Bengali. The frequency of the indigenous dialect/language shows area-wise variation with varied concentration of particular linguistic groups. For example, speakers of Tibetan language dominate Kameng, Pasighat has majority of Minyong speakers (Siang), and the speakers of Gallong language have their highest concentration in Daporijo (Siang) area.

Local Government also varies greatly. The Wanchos and Noctes are ruled by powerful chiefs. The Sherdukpens and Hursos are dominated by aristocratic families. The Nishis, on the other hand, have hardly any traditional organisation. The Adis and the Mishmis are governed by a council of elders, *Kebang* or village council.

The people of Arunachal Pradesh are agriculturists and most of them practice shifting cultivation, commonly knows as *Jhum*. Notion of ownership of land among them varies from group to group. But there is a great deal of emphasis on community control over the use of land.

Available data on religious beliefs and practices show that bulk of the people are followers of either tribal or Hindu religion. There are at least 13 communities which have followers of Christianity as well. They are the Galong, Miju, Mikir, Minyong, Miri, Mishing, Mishmi, Nishi, Nocte, Padam, Pasi, Tagin, Tangam, and the Tangsa. A section of the Noctes have been found to be influenced by Vaishnavism. There are at least 9 communities whose members are Buddhists. They are the Khamba, Khampti, Memba, Monpa, Nocte, Ramo, Sherdukpen, Singpho, and the Tangsa.

The Singphos : Their Origin, History and Distribution

The Singphos constitute one of the smallest endogamous groups inhabiting the Tirap district and some parts of the adjoining Lohit district of Arunachal Pradesh.

Their proper tribal name is 'Ching-po'[8] 'Singpho', being its anglicised spelling. Gait[9] maintains that the meaning of the word 'Singpho' is man. But Waddel[10] observes, 'the word does not mean a Man' as is usually stated. The Burmese call them 'Ka - Chin' or 'Ka - Khyen', in contradiction to their south-western neighbours who call them 'Chins' or 'Khyens'.

The people are Buddhist by religion and belong to the Mongoloid stock. Regarding the language it may be mentioned that most of the dialects spoken by the natives of Arunachal Pradesh belong to the Tibeto-Burman branch of the main Sino-Tibetan family. The dialect used by the group is 'Singpho' but the script is Assamese. During one of the trips in Singpho area, a 55 year old village headman communicated that formerly they had used pali script.

Legends about the origin and migration of the group are many and inconsistent. The most commonly accepted tradition, however, claims that they were formerly inhabitants of Upper Burma.[11] According to their own belief, their original homeland was in the Hukang valley in the north-east of the Patkai ranges. *Hukang* is a Singpho word meaning, 'a fence of human heads' (Hu-human head Kang-fence). It refers to the great massacre of the Singphos by the Burmese. Being obstructed by the Burmese in their southward migration, the Singphos turned, towards the south-east, crossed the Patkai ranges of the Indo-Burmese border, and penetrated into the Brahmaputra valley, around 1793 A.D.

The Singphos were great fighters and had so terrorized the Ahoms that their names were well known in Assam by 1810. Waddel[12] maintains, "They crossed the Patkai range near Dibrugarh and settled on the hills of the Dihing river". Robinson[13] observes, "The Singphos are by far the most powerful tribe bordering on the valley.... The Singphos have for several generations been the terror of the Assamese. They were in the constant habit of making eruptions into the plains, in conjunction with the Moamaris or Mattack by whom they appear to have been first called into Assam. They sometimes proceeded as far as the very capital itself, plundering the temples, laying waste the country, and carrying off the inhabitants into slavery. These several eruptions have won for them the low lands they now occupy ...." Slavery was prominent among them. It was estimated that they and their Burmese kinsmen possessed in 1837 not fewer than a hundred thousand Assamese whom they had carried as slaves. The Doaniyas are the half-breeds with their Assamese slaves, and are found mainly on the lower Dihing near Makum and Margareeta in Assam.[14]

The reference of the Singphos, as inhabitants of the Patkai hills are found in the old Assamese chronicles. It shows that they had close contact with Assam even before the Moamaria rebellion. The Singphos were the most troublesome neighbours on the Sadiya front of Assam. They drove out the khamtis from the low lands under the Patkai hills and occupied the Tangapani, east of Sadiya and on the upper Buri-Dihing in Namrup.

During the first quarter of the nineteenth century the Singphos joined the Burmese in their invasions of Assam. In course of these ravages a large number of Ahom subjects were taken away as slaves. Sometime in the middle of 1825, Captain Neufville, the first British Political Agent of Upper Assam advanced up to Noa-Dhing and evicted the Burmese from the villages of the Beesa and Duffa *Gams*. The Singpho chiefs who were the accomplices fled to the hills. Their villages were destroyed and 3,000 Assamese captives were released. But, many more slaves were concealed. *Beesa Gam* and the other chiefs, however, ultimately surrendered to Captain Neufville. In 1825 Mr. Scott, the Governor General's Agent, visited Sadiya. Sixteen out of the twenty eight Singpho chiefs entered into an agreement to release the captives and remain loyal to the British Government.

The release of 6,000 slaves severely affected the Singpho economy. As a compensation Mr. Scott proposed to establish a regular trade between Assam and the Upper Irraweddy basin which would pass through their hands. It was settled that the Beesa *Gam* should have a general control over the rest of the tribe who had surrendered. The idea of trade, however, never materialised as no active steps were ever taken to develop it. On the other hand, neither the Khamptis nor the Singphos could settle down to agriculture, but spent their time in hunting and catching elephants. Being used to getting the fields tilled by the slaves, the Singpho masters were too proud to stoop to manual labour.

In January, 1843, again a large party of Singphos from Burma attacked the British out-post at Ningru and killed seven men. Simultaneous attacks were made in other spots also. All the Singphos on the Noa and Buri-Dihing joined the revolt. Both the Beesa *Gam* and Ningıula were also suspected of having been accomplices at least. They however, had to surrender soon.

The Government appointed a commission to inquire into the cause of the revolt. It was reported that the main cause of the Singpho insurrection was the loss of slaves. The report concluded that the loss of slaves would soon compel them to settle down to cultivation.

The Singphos gradually reconciled to the loss, gave up the path of hostility and settled in different places as loyal subjects.

At present, they are concentrated in Bordumsa and Miao area in Tirap district in Arunachal Pradesh. According to 1971 census, the total Singpho population in Tirap was 1168 (men 581, women 587). A few of them have also settled in Lohit district of Arunachal Pradesh, and Dibrugarh district of Assam.

Socio-Political and Economic Life

The Singphos practise partrilocal residence and partrilineal descent and inheritance. Polygyny is prevalent. Divorce, re-marriage of divorced woman and widowhood are permitted. Bride price *(Fung-a)* is prevalent. They permit levirate, sororate and filial inheritance (except own mother). Cross-cousin marriage (mother's brother's daughter) is preferred by the people.

The average size of a family is 6. Around 80 p.c. of the families are of nuclear type. Eldest male member is the head of the family. Though an endogamous group, the clans are again divided into sub-clans *(Tingong)* or families. It seems there does not exist any hierarchy in the different clans to regulate inter-marriage. But, the flow of mates between clans takes place single-way.

All the Singpho villages have been brought under the jurisdiction of Anchal Samity and Gaon panchayat administration. But these bodies are mostly preoccupied with programmes concerning regional development. In the affairs of day-to-day social control the traditional organization are of utmost importance to the people.

Shri Beesa-gam Rajkumar is the present Singpho king and is the ex-officio Head of all the traditional bodies. All the people are loyal to him. The office of the king is hereditary.

Every Singpho village has a *Gaon-Bura* (Headman) who is selected by the villagers. Now-a-days, the *Gaon-Bura* has been formally recognised by the Government. A village has a council of elderly people which is led by the *Gaon-Bura.* Knowledge of Singpho tradition and culture is an essential qualification to be a councillor. The main purpose of the council is to keep the village and social life at a useful level of interaction. Violation of social norms with regard to marriage rules and other social usages is also dealt with by the council.

The King, being the chief of all the Singphos acts as a co-ordinator. All the *Gaon-Buras* are loyal to the king. A dispute which cannot be settled by the council is brought before the king whose verdict is obeyed and respected. Inter-village disputes are normally settled by the king in consultation with the respective *Gaon Buras* and other elderly members.

Besides the council of elderly people (Slangboidrare), each Singpho village, traditionally, has two more associations, namely, (a) Mangungbang (association of young boys) and (b) Numsabang (association of young girls). Both these associations mainly look after the welfare activities of the community. These provide the volunteers and manual labourers on the occasions of house construction, marriage and the educated young boys command sufficient respect of the people and even the elderly people seek their advice whenever necessary.

Leadership picture of the community will remain incomplete without a reference to Buddhist Monks. Each Singpho village has a Buddhist monastery called Bapu-chang or *Buddha Vihar* (Buddha temple). The monks of these monasteries command more influence on the people than other political and social leaders. The major socio-religious ceremonies of the people centre around the *Vihar* and the monk's presence is essential in these ceremonies. The people obey him with great reverence and seek solace from him in adversities and crises.

Singphos are generally agriculturists. The important crops of the area are paddy, mustard, maize, potato, wheat and sugarcane. Rice is their staple food. They have given up their traditional habit of living upon wild yams and other jungle products as also hunting and catching elephants. There are, however, a few people who are even now expert in catching elephants from the forest. With the introduction of formal education, a few of them are in service and business. Although agriculture continues to be the main base of their economy, it is interesting to note that generally, the people show reluctance to work in their agricultural land. It may be due to the fact that formerly they used to depend mainly upon the services of slaves for these works. It seems that they are yet to get themselves adapted to the agricultural activities. At present they hire land-less labourers to work for them on share system. Most of the labourers are ex-tea garden labourers and are Nepalis. They are granted residential permits by the local administration for six months at a time. The permit is obtained by their employers and renewed at regular intervals. They are provided with some land by their Singpho masters to construct residential houses where they stay more or less permanently either individually or with their families.

Besides the reasons of history, their aversion to agricultural activities has been attributed by many to their opium addiction. It is difficult to give an accurate statistical figure in terms of number or percentage because most of them do not voluntarily come out with the information, but it may be generally stated, that opium addiction among the Singphos is reasonably high. In many families, it has been reported that the mothers, in order to be able to do household works, provide a moaning child with small dose of opium. Besides in most of the cases, it is started either for relief from excessive exhaustion or pain, or as a cure for dysentery or other stomach troubles.

It may relevantly be noted here that opium addiction is more or less equally endemic among the Noctes and Wanchos of Tirap district. The Government of Arunachal Pradesh is fully aware of the problem and three opium de-addiction units have been opened in Longding (Wancho area), Khonsa (Nocte) and Bordumsa (Singpho), each with ten beds and one medical officer.

The Problem and Some Observations

The various groups inhabiting the Himalayan region represent different ante-cedents and levels of techno-economic development, they differ greatly in their numbers and complexity of social organization and there are wide variations in their customs and institutions. Thus the process of development cannot be a matter of devising a formula or a general scheme for people's development (as against the Regional Development). The group, its overt and covert problems, its history and its traditional socio-political structure need to be understood and appreciated in proper and total perspective.

It has been noted earlier that the Singphos were originally a hill people from Upper Burma. They were a warrior group and used to raid Assam villages very frequently. They were subjugated by the British only during the mid-nineteenth century and were forced to settle down to agriculture, which they apparently did half-heartedly.

Mazindar Barua[15] observes, "In their original home land they practised gathering and chase. Agriculture was crude and a subsidiary occupation, and they had not yet learnt methods of permanent cultivation. Here pursuit of agriculture lessened labour for living and gave them enough of leisure. Through idleness they lost much of their moral and material virtues." He continues, "The Singphos are by nature averse to hard labour and to the plodding regularity of a cultivator's life. In spite of their having plenty of land in the area for opening new fields, they have not concerned themselves to intensive cultivation. They remain content with producing just as much they require, just sufficient to stave off starvation."

Even today, they do not seem to have been properly adapted to the agricultural techniques and way of life and depend on hired labour. This practice leaves some observable impact on their general economic condition. It has been estimated that the per capita yield for the Singphos is at present reduced by an average of 25 to 30 per cent. Besides, in migration of persons from the neighbourhood, if continued uninterrupted, may upset the total balance.

It is necessary that the people should be motivated and oriented towards agricultural activities. Besides motivation through mass media and audo-visual publicity programmes, field instructors should plan door-to-door campaign in phased manner to impart practical training. Economic condition of the Singphos is not likely to improve unless the people themselves till and harvest their land, alongside, some measures need be taken to regulate in-migration. This will indirectly contribute positively to the process of achieving self-reliance.

Once a warrior tribe, the Singphos in the present setting seem to be, in general, very lazy and averse to hard work. It is very difficult to identify with certainty the reasons or this more or less universal lethargy among these people. It is held by many that their habit of opium intake may be an important factor for the same. This habit results in depression and euphoria. An addict suffers form moral depravity, loss of responsibility and will power. It produces a feeling of lethargy and encourages idleness. Gait[16] observes, "Their pacific attitude in recent times is attributed by some to their now universal habit of taking excessive quantities of opium which, it is said, had sapped their energy and robbed them of their old war-like proclivities. Waddel[17] maintains. "In Assam they have degenerated somewhat by opium eating and spirit drinking."

Earlier, they used to get opium from Burma. Since 1960, the supply from Burma has gradually been disrupted. At present, it is obtained form Dibrugarh through some agents inhabiting the nearby villages on Assam frontier.

Among the younger generation, an awareness has been observed about the far-reaching implications of the habit on the group. They believe and probably very rightly, that opium has a degenerating effect on the Singphos as a whole. It seems they are eager to extend all possible help to the Government and other agencies engaged in opium de-addiction programme.

Besides the general health and economic dimensions, the habit seems to have some other very genuine implications also.

The population apparently has been steadily declining since long. Some authorities consider opium addiction to have significantly contributed to the tribe's decreasing fertility and increasing mortality rate also. The medical officers, attached to various Health units in the area are of the opinion that regular intake of opium makes the sensory nerves very ineffective and turns the person gradually very lethargic and very often impotent or near-impotent. Thus, it ultimately may reduce the fertility of the group. Another reason is the endemic malaria disease. The Singpho belt from Bordumsa to Miao was hitherto a malaria prone region. Medical department failed to control the disease by spraying D.D.T. in 1982. Athletic Spray, a substitute for D.D.T. was imported from the U.S.A., to combat the disease. But, it has not yet been fully eradicated. It is urgently felt that necessary measures be taken for the complete eradication of malaria from the belt, and a full-hearted opium de-addiction campaign be launched among the people.

The way in which the present programme of de-addiction by the Government is functioning does not seem to be very productive. The Government do not have any scheme for motivating the people against opium and also to attend the opium units for de-addiction. The people are to attend the units voluntarily. Further, the habit is such deep rooted that even after being de-addicated and released form hospital, a follow-up vigilance measure is needed to prevent the person from being re-addicted in the company of the addicts in the villages. Sometimes the patients are refused admission to the Centre for want of medicines in the hospital stock.

Besides, the supply of opium from clandestine sources is continuing unabated. One day when the author tried to convince a middle-aged Singpho about the evil effects of opium, he retorted, "you people from Dibrugarh are maintaining a steady supply of opium and at the end you are preaching something else. Why don't you stop the supply from there?"

It is suggested that a programme be taken up to motivate the people against opium, to keep vigilance for some days on the de-addicted person and to control the supply of the article. In addition, they need to be motivated to take medical help for such diseases for which they themselves prescribe and use small doses of opium as medicine. Care is also to be taken to see that the health units do not run short of necessary medicines. It may be noted here that the demographic constraint, very often, leads to some psychological problems and generate an environment of mutual distrust. It is detrimental to the cause of regional integration, in particular and national integration in general. Notwithstanding the fact that they acknowledge the adverse effects of opium addiction, most of the people express suspicion about the published census figures with regard to their total population. They believe that the figures have been deliberately understated to serve some ulterior motives of the Government. They maintain that 'under estimation' in census figures is a conscious effort on the part of the Government to deprive them of proper representation in Government jobs and other bodies.

Necessary steps, thus, need be contemplated to restore the group's confidence in itself and also on others. Family planning campaign among the people may be temporarily suspended.

Eligible individuals from the tribe may be involved in census enumeration of Singpho belt.

While discussing the leadership it has been recorded that the king is the Chief of the Singphos. Now-a-days, educated young boys have been found to enjoy sufficient command over the people. On religious front, Buddhist monk is a greatly revered figure in the community. It would, therefore, be advisable that besides the elected members of the Gaon Panchayat, Anchal Samity, and the Gaon Buras, the Singpho king and the elites may be consulted and taken into confidence for introducing any schemes intended for the development of people. Help and co-operation may also be sought from local Buddhist monk when an issue involves social ethos and moral values.

References

1. R.K. Kar, "Tribal Welfare in India : An Anthropologist's Viewpoint" in *Man and Life* 7:1-22 (1961), p. 77.

2. Verrier Elwin, *A New deal for Tribal India*, (New Delhi, Ministry of Home Affairs, Govt. of India, New Delhi, 1963).

3. B.K. Roy Burman, "Anthropological Concepts of Problems of Planning and Research for Social Development" in *Applied Anthropology in India* (ed.) L.P. Vidyarthi. (Allahabad, Kitab Mahal, 1963), p. 47.

4. See Tarak Chandra Das, *The Puruns*, (University of Calcutta, 1945), Lieut. R. Steward, "Notes on Northern Cachar", *Journal of Asiatic Society of Bengal*. Vol. 24 (1885), L.P. Vidyarthi and B.K. Rai, *The Tribal Culture of India*, (Delhi 1977), C.F. Haimendorf, *The Rajgonds of Adilabad*, Book I, (London, 1948).

5. *Dainik Janambhumi* (17 Oct. 1981), *Statistical Handbook of Tirap, Arunachal Pradesh* (1982), B.D. Sharma, *Planning for Tribal Development*, (New Delhi, Prachi Prakashan, 1984).

6. R.K. Kar, "Arunachal Pradesh and Her People", *Vanyajati* 27 (1980), p. 23.

7. *Ibid.*, pp. 23-25.

8. L.A. Waddel, *The Tribes of the Brahmaputra Valley* (Delhi, Sanskaran Prakashan, (Reprint) 1975, original, 1901, p. 40.

9. Edward Gait, *A History of Assam*, Calcutta, Thacker Spink and Co., 1926,

p. 324.

10. Waddel, op.cit., p. 40.
11. Mazindar Barua and Tapan Kumar, *Singphos and their Religion*, Shillong Research Department, Govt. of Arunachal Pradesh, 1977, p. 6.
12. Waddel, *op.cit.*, p. 39.
13. William Robinson, Descriptive Account of Assam, Delhi Sanskaran Prakashan, (reprint), 1975, (original, 1841), p. 375.
14. Waddel, *op.cit.*, pp. 40-41.
15. Barua, *op.cit.*, p. 4.
16. Gait, *op.cit.*, p. 24.
17. Waddel, *op.cit.*, p. 39.

5

Changes in Tibetan Economy, 1959-76

DAWA NORBU

When we talk about the industry in Tibet, we must keep in mind its limited scale which is not to discredit China's industrial effort but to keep a proper perspective. It is true that Tibet had no modern industry before "liberation" but to know why is only to be fair to the ancient regime.

Industry

Modern industry as is well known had its origins in Europe and industrialization in most non-European countries was initiated under the auspices of European colonial rule, or as a result of contacts with Europeans. But Tibet completely escaped European colonialism. The security interests of the British Empire in India dictated that Tibet be made a buffer state and be completely insulated from any foreign contacts. The Lhasa Convention of 1904 signed at Lhasa after the Younghusband "Expedition" and the Anglo-Russian Treaty of 1907 signed at St. Petersburg made sure that no other powers may get into Tibet. And the British themselves, apart from policing the region, would not colonize because it was not worthwhile economically.

But the magical wheel never ceased to fascinate the Thirteenth Dalai Lama (as it does the present Dalai Lama) when he was in exile in India. Charles Bell writes:

> The Tibetans, when in India, liked greatly to visit industrial establishments and factories .... An arsenal and mint were of unfailing interest to them, but little places where silk and cotton goods or gold and silver ornaments were turned out, were also eagerly examined.[1]

In 1914 the Tibetan plenipotentiary to the Simla Conference told Bell that Tibet was interested in developing mines, employing British of Indian engineers, but making it clear that such mines must be under Tibetan ownership.[2] It appears that Britain was not against the Tibetan desires to develop modern industry as long as it was under her auspices. Thus, the British government agreed to help Tibet in obtaining mining prospectors, in importing machinery for mines and mint, to open an English type of School and establish a telegraph line between Gyantse and Lhasa. As a part of this program four boys were sent to England for modern education. But the whole attempt was nipped in its bud by vehement opposition from the powerful monasteries. It is said that Nationalist China bribed and instigated the abbots in Lhasa;[3] slightest instigation was enough.

Despite the undisputed charismatic power of the Dalai Lama over the Tibetan, even the small changes he proposed were resolutely opposed. What this fact proves is that unless industralization is imposed by force it is almost impossible through voluntary effort in a pre-industrial society. In China, India and Japan, initial attempts at industrialization were traumatic experiences.

The present Dalai Lama had a similar dream, but this was cut short by the Chinese Communist "liberation" in 1950. This makes difficult any answer to a question that is often asked: Would the Tibetan ruling class have carried out over due changes, including industrialization, even if the Chinese did not come? The Dalai Lama admitted when I asked him the same question that any attempt, even an honest one, to answer such a question is likely to sound dubious. There is no doubt that he was even more keenly curious about machines than his predecessor was, as is evident from Heinrich Harner's best-seller, *Seven Years in Tibet*. But this does not prove much—objectively. However, when he formally ascended the throne in 1950, he did institute a reform committee (Lekchod Tsogchung).[4] This coincided with the "liberation" and could easily be said, was occasioned by the Chinese. Although Tibet, left to herself, would or could not probably have carried on development on a scale that China has initiated, she would not certainly have remained a closed country any longer hostile to change because of revolutionary changes taking place all around her, including India and China. Nor would she have paid such a high price for development as she has done under the Chinese rule.

Motivation for industrialization in general seems fairly obvious but it is not so simple in the case of Tibet which has been such a controversial political issue in the past. There indeed seems to be such a thing as politics of industrialization. Since industrialization is one of the most sought-after goals of most developing countries, it becomes a handy legitmization device and justification for past immoral or illegal actions. The unlimited propaganda value of even limited industry is enormous as the Chinese attempt in Lhasa demonstrates. The fact that modern industry has been introduced into a pre-industrial society is enough to steal the show; most people would not have a second thought about either its scale or the price of it.

The first group of Tibetan mechanics graduated in China and went back to Tibet in 1963.[5] An iron and steel plant opened in June, and a vehicle accessories workshop in October.[6] By 1964 there were reportedly over 50 small and medium sized factories in Tibet, of which 20 were located in Lhasa.[7] A year later the number of factories has risen to 67.[8]

Chinese publications always make a reference to 1959 (since the Rebellion) and 1965 (beginning of the Cultural Revolution) as turning points in Tibet's modern history. Before 1954 there was no industry in TAR, although the Chinese came in 1950. Industry in Tibet is said to have mushroomed progressively since these two important dates. Lhasa Radio of May 28, 1974 provides a typical official assessment of the present industrial situation in Tibet:

> Under the wise leadership of the Party and Chairman Mao and as a result of democratic reforms after liberation, and especially during the great proletarian cultural revolution, industry in Tibet has been built from scratch and has rigorously grown in scale. At present the region has several hundred medium-sized and small factories and mines including electric power, fuel, chemical, machinery, mining, construction, paper-making, printing and power plants, 70% of which were built and developed during the Cultural Revolution. The output of major products including coal, electric power, cement, agricultural machinery and building material increased from two to several times (compared with that before the Cultural Revolution). Self-sufficiency has been achieved in timber, coal, matches, sulfuric acid, woolen fabrics, woolen yarn, woolen blankets, leather and edible oil and some surplus products have supported fraternal provinces.[9]

A year later *New China News Agency* released a somewhat clearer report on the industrial situation in Tibet. It said that Tibet has now "more than" 250 industrial and mining enterprises, and recalling that in 1965 there were only 80 factories and mines. In 1974 industry accounted for 22% of the region's total output value as against 8% in 1955.[10] By 1975, Tibet had "begun to export wool and woolen products ...."[11] It should be noted that in all its progress reports, China very seldom mentions the exact total production figures. Necessary increase is always indicated by percentages, giving figures neither for the current year nor for the base year.

The most publicized and therefore the best known factory in entire Tibet in Linchih (actually Ngimed) Woolen Textile Factory. Built from a plant moved form Shanghai in 1964 and also with Chinese workers form the same city, it started production in January 1967 and by 1970 had a new woolen yarn workshop the size of the original factory. In 1975 the factory was employing 1500 workers and producing 250 different products including woolen pieces goods, blankets, and yarn.[12]

The Chinese textile enterprise in Tibet should be successful because Tibet must be one of the major wool producing areas in China now. Before the "liberation" Tibet's major export item was wool. As we shall see with the organization of the animal husbandry, wool output has increased considerably.

Another natural endowment in Tibet is the number of mountain streams, particularly suited for power generation. Lhasa had a hydro-electric power station before the Chinese coming, and in 1956 the city was electrified by a 600 kilowatt hydro-electric power plant. Another power station of 7500 kw went into operation by April 1960. By 1971, about 100 small and medium-sized hydro-electric stations serving more than half of Tibet's administrative units had been constructed. (By this it is probably meant, as indeed Tibetan refugee accounts testify that the Chinese administrative offices at various levels have been electrified and not the countryside). It was reported that power output by 1970 was double that of 1965.[13] Apart from the electrification of the region, water power resources and coal mines have apparently been able to help overcome the scarcity of fuel and power which hampered industrialization. Besides, a battery plant completed in 1971 makes Tibet self-sufficient in the product.

Recent Chinese researchers have disclosed that they have discovered about 21 different kinds of minerals such as iron ore, copper, borax, graphite,sulphur,gold. But full exploration of minerals is yet to be undertaken or yet to be disclosed. Soon after the Lhasa Revolt in March 1959 a backyard blast furnace that acquired the sanctity and futility of a ritual throughout China during the Leap Forward period was erected in Lhasa. Its capacity was one and a half tones of pig iron, using local ore and coal. The Wuli coal mine north of Lhasa, discovered and operated by the PLA units in the area, was supposedly meeting the fuel needs of the local areas. In 1964 an ordinance factory began producing ammunition at a place about 2 miles east of Lhasa near Sera Monastery with electricity supplied by Naichin hydro-electric project,[14] on the banks of Kyi-Chu River. Tibet is however, the only region in China which does not have a steel industry.

Other industrial items that find repeated mention in the Chinese press are tanneries, canneries, dairies and other food processing factories that began in 1960 in the Lhasa suburbs.[15] The Lhasa Pharmacological Factory produces serum for animals and the cement plant in the same city produces building material from locally-available coal, clay, and lime.[16]

The traditional Tibetan handicrafts, reorganized and improved, constitutes the greater part of modern industry in Tibet today. If modern industry is restricted to Lhasa and its vicinity, cottage industry is found in most Tibetan towns such as Lhasa, Gyantse, Shigatse, etc. Between 1960-62 artisans in Lhasa increased over 500. NCNA reported in 1976 that producers' cooperatives with state financial and technological assistance began in 1966 and since then have been increasing. By the end of 1975 some 400 handicraft cooperatives, in 18 trades including textiles, tanning, tailoring, ironware and pottery had been established. As a result of the reorganization the total output is said to have increased by 2.28 over the year 1965.[17]

According to Chinese reports the Central government has been giving considerable subsidies and technical assistance for the industralization of Tibet. A NCNA report of 18 March 1975 said that a "preferential policy in taxation and commodity pricing" was introduced in the early 1960s and that central subsidies to Tibet had accounted for more than 90% of its total expenditure. In the first quarter of 1974 supply of material and equipment by the State into Tibet increased by 102% and 31% increase in the amount of material in support of agriculture and animal husbandry.[18]

Although it makes economic sense to render such central economic assistance in order to close the regional imbalance in development, there should be enough resources, financial or otherwise, in Tibet itself. One can think of two major sources of capital for Tibetan industrialization. First, all the gold and silver objects and other precious stones confiscated form the ruling class during the "democratic reforms" were not distributed to the poor; they were kept aside for future developmental projects.[19] The value of such precious property is enormous when we remember that in Tibet most of the economic surplus and capital savings were converted into such valuables. Further, most of the socially-accumulated Tibetan wealth of the last 1000 years used to be in monasteries in the form of gold, silver, and other precious metallic icons.

Second, both agricultural and dairy outputs have definitely increased but the rationing scale has not, as we shall see later. This raises the question, as indeed *The Guardian* (London) did a couple of years ago, as to where the economic surplus goes.[20] Tibet was very much self-sufficient in food even before the "liberation".

If in the past the number of monks or lamas was seen by the orthodox as an index of the religiosity of Tibet, the new regime considers the number of industrial workers (Proletariat) as a measure of revolutionary progress towards socialism. But most of the so-called industrial workers are mobilized handicraftsmen.[21] For example, one third of the population in Lhasa (40,000 approx) where most of the industries are located, are reported to be industrial workers, which includes the handicraft workers numbering 6,000. Most of the skilled workers are Chinese, but Tibetans are gradually being trained in industrial skills. It was reported that in 1961 there were 24,000 workers.[22] In 1968 there were 26,000 industrial workers and 8,000 of them were declared as qualified lathe turners, fitters and welders.[23] In 1975 it was reported that about 10,000 Tibetans had been trained in mining, and other technical vocations in various Chinese cities. Moreover, the local work-force is assisted and trained by workers and technicians from all over China.[24] The total industrial work force was reported to be 67,000 in 1975.[25]

It appears that Tibetans do not constitute more than half of the industrial working class, being about four per cent of Tibet's population.[26] In 1973 two-thirds of the skilled workers in the Tumenkola coal mine were Tibetans; and 70% of the construction workers.[27] At the Second Tibet Trade Union Congress held in Lhasa in August, 1973 only 50% of the delegates and 65% of the members of its committee were Tibetans.[28] In the same year out of 1300 postal workers only 30% were Tibetans.[29]

The Chinese press was ecstatic about the recent discovery of coal in Tibet. In 1972 there were sixteen small coal mines and two years later coal output had increased by 150% over that of 1965. Many of these mines started by using "indigenous methods", a fact that contradicts Chinese claims that they had introduced iron tools into Tibet. Machinery is also used for mining although on a small scale.[30] In 1972 a mass movement was launched to find coal and other mineral deposits.

Agriculture

It is commonly accepted that Chinese have made more judicious use of force than their Russian comrades did. In Tibet, whatever development there exists is largely due to the Chinese organisational skill and their mobilization of the people. It is, therefore, proper that we preface our examination of the economic development in Tibet by the mobilization of a population that had hitherto remained immobile.

Almost immediately after the 1959 Revolt, about 10-11 households were organized into mutual aid teams modeled on the Chinese lines. In China the next stage of the organisational development was the establishment of producers' cooperatives. By 1961 over 90% of peasant households merged into 22,000 mutual aid teams, embracing 166,000 households.[31] In most parts of Tibet, this intermediary stage seemed to have been skipped over; a few places like Chiepa and Naitung, however, underwent this stage as well. Later mutual aid teams in Chiepa and Naitung, which are described as pioneers merged into an agricultural producers' cooperative. By 1966 this cooperative became a part of a people's commune consisting of 2,000 households.[32]

The first communes were set up on a trial basis in 1965 and subsequently extended "step by step". By the end of the year 130 communes were established and by September 1975, the communization was practically complete: 99% of the townships in Tibet were said to be covered by communes.[33]

It would appear both from Chinese reports and Tibetan refugee accounts that communes were based on former townships. A Tibetan commune is therefore smaller both in population and area than the Chinese counterparts. It also appears that it is organized on a dual basis — commune and production team rather than on the Chinese customary triple basis of communes, brigades, and production teams. Communes have been largely responsible for the increased agricultural output.

Tibetan economy had been in the past — and still remains — essentially an agricultural economy with a significant pastoral sector that comprises about one-third of the whole. Barley, which is the staple diet in Tibet, accounts for roughly one-third of all agricultural land and two-thirds of the area given to crops. Other important crops are wheat, green peas and millet. Soon after the 1959 revolt land was distributed equally to all but only to be collectivized six years later. By April 1960 over 186,000 hectares of land was distributed to 1000,000 peasant households.[34]

Agriculture, therefore, has naturally received a great deal of attention form the Chinese central and local authorities, as to be expected. With their experience in dealing with peasant problems, the Communists have organized the loose structure of the Tibetan economy as never before on the Chinese model and mobilized the Tibetan peasantry that used to be allergic to any organization for continuous hard labour and increased production. As we have already discussed the details of mass mobilization, it is important to emphasize here the fundamental contribution that these "subjective" factors have made to the overall income in agricultural output that China publicizes year after year. Since the spring of 1973 there has been even greater stress on these factors with the launching of an intensive campaign to "learn form Techai" and "Catch Up with Leihmai" (the latter being Tibet's own agricultural model). In late 1974 the hero of Tachai along with a delegation of Chinese model farmers visited Tibet and held a conference on "learning From Tachai" there.

It is evident that the Chinese have met strong resistance from the Tibetan peasantry which, unlike the Chinese counterpart, was never mobilized until after the Tibetan Revolt. Tibetan refugees during the late 1960s and early 1970s persistently complained against the introduction of commune which made them work harder and which closed all other small sources of food which were available before and left the peasantry with the only officially sanctioned ration. Above all, they seemed to have resented the fact and feeling of being subjected structurally and organizationally so ruthlessly efficient, driving system that they have never before experienced. "Through these organisations they made us work or sleep, sing or cry, just as the Almighty Party wanted".[35] Such complaints become understandable when we keep in mind the extremely loose peasant organization that existed before the Chinese takeover, not withstanding the feudal system. Thus, Robert Bardley, one of the editors of *The Wall Street Journal* who visited Lhasa in late 1976 commented:

> It is patently absurd for the People's Republic of China to talk of serfdom. Land is much more effectively owned by the State today than it was ever owned by the Dalai Lama; peasants can no more leave communes than they could leave their manor.[36]

The Chinese mass media, of course, would not openly admit such peasant resistance to regimentation. Even then we can observe sufficient evidence in between the official lines, to confirm what we have suggested. An American researcher, after having surveyed the recent economic developments concluded that "warnings and exhortations were directed at agricultural work in general to such an extent that one cannot escape the conclusion that some serious problems had arisen."[37] In the fall of 1971 it was reported that new planting methods had been opposed by some "unreformed landlords and compradors."[38] Other reports warn the people against "wandering about, sticking to old ways, pushing backward, relying on a small group of people or on getting more equipment than labour."[39] One can go on quoting such examples but the point seems clear; it would be naive to expect that Chinese, even with their proverbial revolutionary zeal and organizational abilities, can change the habits and attitudes of the peasantry formed over centuries, within a decade or two.

Resistance or no resistance to change, the "production mentality" reigns supreme. Peasants are mobilized to work harder and increase production. This is done in two main ways, apart from the usual intensive labour input : irrigation and reclamation of wastelands that abound in a continental plateau with sparse population. An improved irrigation system is particularly welcome to an area that receives minimal rainfall. Chinese claims seem to imply that irrigation was almost non-existent before, which is of course not true, though it was probably inadequate for higher consumption. It was reported that by 1971 "more than 80% of Tibet's cultivated area was under irrigation."[40] But in late 1974 the same sources disclosed that 70% of Tibetan farmland was irrigated. "This however, does not represent an increase over 1964."[41] Between 1959 and 1966 the total acreage under irrigation increased by 30%, while the newly-irrigated farmland comprised only "nearly" 1000,000 hectares for the whole region.

Although the Chinese publications describe many land reclamation projects, figures are seldom given for the total increase in arable land. However, an Indian scholar quotes a figure of

56,000 hectares of marginal lands reclaimed for cultivation during the past decade.[42]

In 1975 it was predicted that agriculture in Tibet would be completely mechanised by 1980,[43] probably following the suggestion made at the "Learn from Tachai" Conference on Agriculture, on the need for farm mechanization. We can however rule out safely any significant role played by mechanization in the past in increasing the agricultural outputs in Tibet. The basic mode of production remains essentially the same as before. The pictures of farm tractors that we see often in glossy Chinese magazines are more for propaganda than for production, when concerning Tibet as a whole.

The real contribution that modern science has so far made in the Tibetan countryside is in simpler but more practical terms of new farming techniques, based more on common sense than on science. In 1974 the Chinese press was filled with reports of scientific findings by Chinese research team that conducted field research into the various aspects of agriculture on the Tibetan plateau since 1973. Composed of 20 categories of specialists from the Chinese Academy of Sciences and from similar local institutions in Tibet, the team conducted useful research into land reclamation, forestry and water conservancy and even more useful scientific data. Peking Radio broadcast on May 7, 1974 said that the team offered local authorities advice on the possibility of rice, wheat and tea growing in Tibet. The aim of the field research was

> To determine the history of the geological development of this plateau, to analyse the influence of its elevation on the natural environment and on human activities, to study the features of its natural conditions and resources, and to discover means to transform and use it.[44]

There have also been less ambitious researches conducted by the Tibet Research Institute of Agricultural Science and Tibet Meteorological Bureau. The Tibetan Plateau averaging more than 4,000 meters above sea level, has short frost-free period and low mean temperature. Such a climate is generally unfavourable to agricultural production. However, there are favourable conditions too. In Lhasa January mean temperature is about two degrees below zero, the lowest being 16.5 degrees below zero. This compares favourably with the January mean temperature of four to eight degrees below zero in North China's winter wheat growing areas. Besides, other favourable conditions include : long length of day, low humidity and strong sunshine, longer warm period, big temperature difference between day and night and fairly ample supply of water. [It should be noted that this area (Lhasa) was well-known for it productivity even in ancient times. Known as the "granary of Tibet", Southern Tibet was the cradle of Tibetan civilization where earliest known dynasties had their origins. River Tsangpo or Brahmaputra flows through this area].

These findings have, however, led to interesting agricultural experiments which have received some attention from the Chinese mass media recently. The Tibetan Institute of Agricultural Science and Shigatse Agricultural Experiment Farm have developed eight strains of wheat and five strains of barley which are resistant to drought and cold. In short, they are suitable for the Tibetan soil and climate. In late 1974 the Chinese press reported that in 21,300 hectares winter wheat had been planted, an event that was hailed throughout China as the Green Revolution was in India.[45] A year later it was reported that 50 countries had started to grow winter wheat on a total of 46,000 hectares of land. Some young Tibetan refugees who were formerly working for the Chinese Administration in Lhasa say that wheat growing is mostly concentrated in Lhasa and Loka areas. They also point out that most of the winter wheat growing farms are PLA-run farms and state farms. It is the same fertile areas and may be the same state farms in some cases that the Chinese claim "double cropping". The fact is, even before liberation, "lands near Lhasa yielded six times the amount of seed sown in normal years."[46]

NCNA reported on successes in double and triple cropping wheat at an average altitude of 4,000 meters. The 1975 harvest of the region (Lhoka?) was reported be 8% more than it was the previous year, which is better than the estimated national increase of 7.5%, for the same year.

Like in the case of industrial output, no figures are given to express agricultural progress. The necessary increase in output is always expressed in percentages. However, on the basis of certain figures that the Chinese favoured to give to two English visitors to Lhasa in 1961, Ann Holmes has worked out the following production figures for barley.[47]

Table 1

Year	*Million Catties*
1958	300
1959	350
1960	420
1961	450
1962	450
1963	480

The celebration of the Tenth Anniversary of the Tibetan Autonomy in September 1975 occasioned an official stock-taking and recitation of progress by big percentages without mentioning any figures for the base or current year. The grain output during the period 1965-1974 increased by 48% and the number of animals by 25%. If this is true, the annual increase in grain output of 4.8% is above the national average which was only 4% over a twenty-five year period[48] (1949-1974).

Although increasing agricultural output is self-evident, it becomes more difficult to see where the surplus goes. As far as rationing is concerned, there has been no increase since 1959.[49] The matter becomes even more complicated when we hear of the Chinese claims of lower taxation, State subsidies and other material assistance to the area; that local taxes contribute only 8.4% of the Region's revenue; that the Central Government spends four times the amount of tax collected from Tibet on the regional development projects; that the State provided 30% of the grain consumed between 1960-1974.[50] The Chinese press, however, in 1973 reported that the State collected 11 million catties of grain and 1.1 million in taxes. Tibet had become self-sufficient in food for the first time in 1974.[51]

Now all these reports of ever-growing prosperity contradict all that the Tibetan refugees say they have experienced in Tibet. It must be mentioned that refugees crossing the Himalayan borders during the late 1960s and early 1970s which coincided with the mass introduction of communes throughout Tibet mention the scarcity of food as one of the main reasons for leaving Tibet. In order to understand such complaints we must know some basic facts which neither China nor her friends ever mention. Rationing introduced in late 1959 which has no precedence in Tibetan history, has not increased at all, as already noted. The monthly quotas for four grades of labourers are as follows: 22, 24, 26 and 28 *gyama*.[52] Since the State applied the socialist principle " "He who does not work, neither shall he eat, and "from each according to his ability, to each according to his work," as enshrined in the Chinese Constitution,[53] people who suffer most economically are those families with many children, aged parents, or infirm. Such families are more than normal in contemporary Tibet because a considerable proportion of the able-bodied population, male in particular, died during the Revolt and most refugees tend to be comparatively young.

On the other hand, the number of what Tibetan refugees call "sweet-sounding taxes" have increased : *Son-Kyin* (seeds debt); gyalche chidru (national tax 7.5%); *dru-lak pue-tsong* ("surplus" grains for sale to the State); *mimang chi-khang zuk-turn* (contribution to commune development projects); *mog-gyab dra-dig kajug* (get ready for war reserve). In other words, grain minus the ration quota is collected by the State for supposedly various purposes. It must be emphasized here again that these down-to-earth facts never find their way in the Chinese press, and yet they are what really matter to the peasant in his daily life. It should also be remembered that China publishes figures, if and when it does at all, of nothing less than the very best, which is of course exceptional rather than the average. In 1974 the figures for the members of Tibet's "Tachai" (agricultural model) Leihmai were published, and any attempt to draw conclusion on the basis of such exceptional figures is not only likely to be unrepresentative, but also unfair.

But the mystery remains. The *Guardian* n 1975 carried a special full-paged report on the current situation in Tibet and wondered about the missing surplus which the report said remains a "mystery".[54] Chinese claim that Tibet became self-sufficient in food in 1974 is incredible; Tibet was self-sufficient in food even before the Chinese came. It is a historical fact none of the poor economic conditions that plagued the Chinese peasantry before "liberation" prevailed in Tibet.

> It is a historical fact, confirmed by Western travellers, that Tibet experienced no famine in her recorded history. It is also a historical fact that there had been no peasant rebellions, which might suggest poverty or some gross injustice.[55]

If we accept that China provided 30% of the grain consumed between 1970 and 1974, we have difficulty in imagining what sort of grains the State supplied to Tibet, because there is no barley growing region (which is the Tibetan staple diet) in China apart from Tibet. It might be argued that China could have supplied rice or cereals, though none of the refugees I have met remember eating other than tsampa.[56] What really seems to have happened is that Chinese publicists have created a deliberate ambiguity which we can figure out.

It cannot be denied that agricultural production has increased, though not perhaps as much as China would have us believe, that the peasants get nothing more than the sanctioned ration, especially after communization which reinforced a tighter control; and that the State continues to collect its taxes. The NCNA report in 1973 quoted earlier, stated that the State collected 11 million catties of grain and 1.1 million in taxes in Tibet. Therefore there can be three possible explanations: (1) transport the surplus to China which seems economically unfeasible; (2) feed the PLA and other Chinese civilians totalling 120,000[57] in Tibet, which is not implausible; (3) use it for the development of Tibet, which is what they should be doing.

Now, the deliberate ambiguity seems to be this: when China says that the State provided the Tibetan people 30% of the grain they consumed between 1960 and 1974, it could mean that the 30%, if the figure is accurate, actually comes from Tibet itself and not from China, as the Chinese reports seeks to imply, assuming the various "sweet-sounding' taxes are kept within the Region, which to me seems to be a fair assumption. If we accept this assumption, then we cannot rule out the explanations (2) and (3). The other important implications are that if the State sold or loaned 30% of the grains consumed for the last 15 years, it would mean that the official ration quota for Tibetans falls short by 10% because ration quotas according to work points are always given everywhere in Tibet usually immediately after the autumn harvest. It would mean most probably that those households with too many mouths to feed and too few hands to work are compelled to purchase or get loans form the State that collects Tibet's surplus.

Animal Husbandry

Before 1951 about one-sixth of Tibet's total population was estimated to be engaged in pastorialism or livestock breeding. Chinese reports say specifically 200,000 nomads. The Chinese press reported that by April 1960, animals, mostly yaks and sheep, owned by the ruling elite but raised by nomads were turned over to 4,800 poor shepherds. But this report is questionable because a special policy called *Broglas Sridjus* (policy directive on work among nomads) was carried out. The animals were not distributed equally among nomads in the way the property and land of the upper classes were distributed among the poor peasants. The shepherds were told to keep and look after "their" animals as before but warned that no animal may be slaughtered without permission. The reason seems clear. If flocks were fragmented, it would be difficult for the Party to keep track of animals which must not be slaughtered for obvious reasons. So democratic reforms, though ideologically tempting, were brushed aside as uneconomical among the nomads. In any case it was a matter of five or six years before collectivization. In fact, soon after the 1959 Revolt Chinese declared that "no-live-stock breeders' cooperative will be established in Central Tibet for the next five years." In fact, Chang Ching-u gave the following assurance:

> Since conditions in the pastoral areas differ from those in the rural areas there will be no struggle meetings, no redistribution of livestock, no differentiation by classes and a policy of mutual benefit between livestock owners and herdsman will be carried out. This is for the purpose of giving full play to the initiative of the livestock owners in managing animal husbandry.[58]

However, in their endeavour to increase production Chinese tried to introduce some elementary organization into the nomadic world that knew no organization. In Eastern Tibet which was considered *de jure* China, even before 1950, the policy of "fixed abodes and nomadic herding" was persued as early as 1958. Because such fixations involved changes in the heardsman's habit of production and way of life, China encountered "severe resistance initially."[59] In Kuchung commune in Western Tibet more than a hundred mud-brick dwellings were constructed to settle the nomadic herdsmen. Similar programmes in other parts of Tibet were also reported.[60]

There have also been reports about how the Chinese are trying to rationalize the better use of pasture. They have ordered the nomads to regularly graze lower pastoral lands in winter, remote upland pastures in summer and fall, and delay migration to winter and spring pastures.

Because of weather, terrain and tradition animal husbandry will on the whole "continue to take first place in planning, with an eye to developing agriculture to its full potential." This was the theme of a congress of advanced collective and producers held at Nokchu Region, an area where China has been more successful in taming the nomads. The conference drew plans for further development of agriculture and livestock. Reports would suggest that progress in animal breeding has not been as dramatic as in agriculture. In 1975 it was reported that livestock increased by 25% for the period 1965-1974 whereas agriculture showed an increase of 48% for the same period.[61] The tax was fixed at 150 gm of wood per taxable sheep which is the standard of taxation for other animals. Contradictory figures on livestock have been given in the past.[62]

This slow pace of progress probably reflects the difficulties that Communists encounter in dealing with nomads who differ vastly from docile peasants; for otherwise, it is most unlikely that the production-minded Communists would have neglected the pastoral economy which is the second most important sector.

An Indian publication, *National Integration*, in its special issue on Tibet in 1964, wrote that nomads posed one of the biggest dilemmas for China in Tibet:

> Even when the first steps at 'reforms' were taken, the official slogan promised "no struggle, no division (distribution) and no class distinction." Later attempts to get tough and exert pressure on the nomads, such as division of water in the grassland areas, establishment of control over the outlets through which the nomads sold their products or obtained grain to supplement their diet of meat and milk products failed miserably. Peking painfully realised that the nomads were sturdily independent, basically self-sufficient and could exist

for long periods without outside help.

The attempt to disrupt the economic structures of the nomads was frustrated by the fact that the line between the rich and poor was narrow and one that was easily crossed by industrious and lucky herd tenders who frequently became herd owners themselves. The lure for "fixed dwelling" only partially succeeded; for though it provided veterinary care for the cattle and help in producing supplementary winter food for the livestock, it destroyed the economic independence of the nomads and made the dictates of alien rulers.[63]

References

1. Charles Bell : *Tibet Past and Present* (London : Oxford University Press, 1968), p. 159.
2. Ibid., pp. 158-59.
3. The author was told by an aristocrat whom I shall not quote as requested.
4. The various measures and programs of the Reform Committee are in documents available with the author.
5. *China Reconstructs* No. 8, (July 1959), pp. 30-31.
6. *Survey of Mainland China Press* (SCMP), No. 2365, (October 19, 1960), p. 22.
7. *Peking Review*, No. 7 (December 18, 1964).
8. *Peking Review*, No. 8 (September 10, 1965), p. 26.
9. *Lhasa Radio*, (May 28, 1974).
10. *NCNA*, (September 9, 1975).
11. *NCNA*, (October 5, 1976).
12. *NCNA*, (March 18, 1975).
13. *Peking Review*, No. 29, (July 16, 1970), p.22.
14. *The Statesman*, (Calcutta, July 2, 1964), p. 6.
15. *China News Service*, (September 17, 1974).

16. *Great Changes in Tibet* (Peking : Foreign Languages Press, 1971) p. 38.
17. *NCNA*, (October 5, 1976).
18. *Lhasa Radio*, (April 22, 1975).
19. See, Dawa Norbu, *Red Star Over Tibet*, (New Delhi; Sterling, 1987), pp. 197-202.
20. *The Guardian*, (London, June 11, 1976).
21. Robert A. Scalapino (ed.) *Elites in Communist China* (Washington: University of Washington Press, 1972,) p. 432.
22. *Communist China and Tibet*, p. 154.
23. *The Times* (London, May 17, 1965).
24. *NCNA*, (September 9, 1975).
25. *NCNA*, (September 8, 1975).
26. Anne Wyman Holmes, *An Examination of the Chinese Occupation of Tibet*, (M.A. Thesis submitted to the University of Oregon, 1976).
27. *Peking Review*, No. 12, (October 10, 1969), p. 25.
28. *FBIS, LTRS*, (July 3, 1973).
29. *Peking Review*, No, 18, (May 2, 1975), pp. 30-31.
30. *SMCP*, No. 5633, (May 31, 1974), p. 115.
31. *SMCP*, No, 2830, (October 2, 1962), p. 22.
32. *Peking Review*, No. 13, (July 31, 1970), p. 30.
33. *NCNA*, (September 10, 1975).
34. *SMCP*, No. 2471, (April 7, 1961).
35. Dawa Norbu, "The Tibetan Response to Chinese Liberation" in *Asian Affairs*, Vol. 62, (October 1975), p. 271.
36. *The Wall Street Journal*, (October 5, 1976).
37. Anne Wyman Holmes, *op.cit.* p. 126.
38. *FBIS, LTRS*,(November 24, 1971).
39. *FBIS, LTRS*, (June 28, 1973; July 18, 1973; June 26, 1973)
40. *People's Daily*, (May 25, 1966); NCNA (Lhasa, March 19, 1966).
41. Anne Wyman Holmes, *op.cit.* p. 178.

42. Pradyumna P. Karan, *The Changing Face of Tibet* (Kentucky : The University Press of Kentucky, 1976), p. 37.

43. *FBIS, LTRS,* (November 3, 1975).

44. *Peking Radio,* (May 7, 1974).

45. *SMCP,* No. 5743, (November 15, 1974), p. 158.

46. Karan, *op.cit.* p. 40.

47. Anne Wyman Holmes, *op.cit.,* p. 104.

48. *NCNA* (May 10, 1975).

49. This is evident from all refugee reports that I came across between 1972-1976 when I was editing the *Tibetan Review*. It is true that there has been no increase in ration quotas in China too.

50. See, *SCMP,* No. 5564, (February 20, 1974), p. 21, and also No. 5726, (October 16, 1974), p. 89.

51. *FBIS, LTRS,* (November, 21, 1973).

52. Gyama = 1 lb. approx.

53. The Constitution of the People's Republic of China adopted in 1975.

54. *The Guardian,* (London, June 6, 1975).

55. *Tibetan Review,* (October-November 1974), p. 4.

56. *Tsampa* is parched barley ground into powder, like flour, and it is the Tibetan staple diet.

57. See Robert Barley's article on Tibet in *The Wall Street* Journal, (September 22, 1976).

58. *SMCP,* No. 2635, (December 8, 1961).

59. Karan, *op.cit.* p. 43.

60. *China Pictorial,* No. 6 (1971), p. 27.

61. *NCNA,* (September 8, 1975).

62. Anne Wyman Holmes, *op.cit.,* p. 114.

63. Gopal Singh (ed.), *National Integration : Tibet Issue* (published by the editor in New Delhi, 1964), p. 18.

6

Problems of Economic Development in Bhutan

MANAS DAS GUPTA

Bhutan was secluded from the rest of the world till 1961. This was a self-imposed isolation.[1] This isolation came to an end only with the beginning of planned development since 1961 under King Jigme Wangchuke, who ascended the throne in 1952. It was only in 1961 the first highway linked central Bhutan with the Indian plains. The road network has since been extended to other parts of the country, replacing foot trails and mule tracks as the principal arteries of commerce and travel. Electricity, telephones, modern schools and hospitals largely unheard of before 1960, are now available at least in the urban and semi-urban areas. Bhutan joined the United Nations in 1971, became the one hundred and forty third members of the I.M.F. in 1981, Asian Pacific Postal Union in 1983 and it has also signed Law of The Sea Convention.

In February 1983 Bhutan's airline began to operate regular services between Calcutta and Paro in central Bhutan. It has become a member of the SAARC and other similar movements. Bhutan's seclusion is thus, a thing of the past. Modernisation process started an accelerated development after 1961. Hence history of Bhutan's modernisation process and economic development are of comparatively recent origin.[2]

Bhutan's Population : "The Least Populated Region"

According to the I.M.F. Survey Report in 1984[3] Bhutan's population is estimated to be just over one million which makes the country the "least populated in the region" (population per sq. km. is 28 in Bhutan compared with 640 in Bangladesh in the same period). The population is predominantly rural with only two townships containing more than 20,000 inhabitants and the rest is scattered in its numerous valleys. Only 3 per cent of population live in the urban areas and 97 per cent in the rural clusters.[4] The distribution of population in Bhutan bears close relationship to physical aspects of land, climatic varieties, degree of the slop of land, and productivities of land. Rural settlements in Bhutan vary largely and widely in size and morphology from a compact group of 20 or more to settlement clusters of about 50 or 100. The dwellings cluster together because of climatic condition, mountain slopes and gradient of mountains. There are about 3454 such villages in Bhutan each having less than 500 population.[5]

Population in the region is relatively sparse. A large section of people are farmers. The economy in many parts is pastoral. This pastoral economy does not allow the concentration of productive resources in a single locality. For this some regions are based on "trans-humance". The raising of livestock is an essential facet of the economy and its importance increases in proportion to altitude. Sheep and goats become more numerous as the height exceeds 10,000 ft. The breeding of yak begins at this elevation. The yak breeding necessiates continuous movement of at least part of population to high pastures. This is facilitated by the possession of alternative houses within easy reach of grazing ground about the tree-line. Yak butter being an important nutrient in the local diet and Buddhist ceremonies, yaks play a very important factor in Bhutan's economy.[6] (According to rough estimate of the Department of Animal Husbandry, Government of Bhutan, in 1980 the population of local cattle was about 1,16,000 that of improved cattle was about 24,000 yak about 26,000 and mule about 24,000). Pastoral economy in Bhutan is as important as the agriculture in Bhutan.

In spite of the progress in modernisation process,[7] Bhutan's economy remains traditional, with subsistence agriculture and animal husbandry contributing a large part of the gross domestic product. Gross Domestic Product (GDP) in 1984 is estimated about 1500 million ngultrum and per capita income is equivalent to $ 125 — one of the lowest in the world. Agriculture and animal husbandry account for one-half of the domestic product, forestry for about 15 per cent, industry and mining for 5 per cent and miscellaneous services for about 30 per cent.[8]

According to the *I.M.F. Survey Report*, the birth rate is about 43.6 per cent per thousand population and death rate of 20.5 per thousand population. The rate of growth of population is estimated to be about 2.3 per cent per annum. The expectation of life at birth of males is 42.2 years and that of females is 45 years.[9] It should be mentioned that since 1950 the population growth rate has never exceeded 1 (one) per cent in Europe and has seldom exceeded 1.5 per cent in North America. The growth rate of population in Bhutan after modernisation process is slightly higher than the average rate of growth of LDC countries, namely 2.0 per cent in the post 1970 period. And the population of Bhutan is growing by more than 2 per cent per annum so that GDP growth of more than 2 per cent is merely a preliminary step before they can start to improve per capita income. According to the World Bank Report the rate of growth of GDP is around (0.2) percent during the 1972-81 in Bhutan.[10]

There are different ethnic groups in Bhutan. The predominant Tibetan Mongoloid groups live in the great Himalaya valleys in the northern and central part of the kingdom. The Nepali settlers are found mostly in the southern region and this group according to conservative estimate is more than 25 per cent of the population.[11] With the beginning of planned development and road construction import of Nepali labourers in power and other projects has led to various social and political tensions.[12]

Thus, Bhutan's development policy has some inherent contradictions. For development Bhutan needs skilled manpower and unskilled workers. This labour force is only available in the neighbouring countries like India and Nepal. But large scale immigration of labourers may to a great extent disrupt the existing ethnic and religious structure. This is what Bhutan wants to avoid. Therefore, the problem of development is likely to be a difficult one. Nepali immigration, legal or illegal remains a problem of Bhutan for a long period. According to one estimate there are about 50,000 Nepali immigrants in Bhutan without proper status and citizenship. The problem is particularly acute in the southern part of Bhutan.[13]

The rulers of Bhutan have always been concerned with the management of kingdom's ethnic relations. These had become very complex and instead of remaining a localised social problems, had entered into the state structure as well.[14]

Important Priority in Bhutan's Development Policy : Investment in Human Capital

The term human capital formation refers to the process of acquiring and increasing the number of persons who have skills, education and experience, which are critical for the economic development of a country. The notion of investment in human capital is of recent origin. In the process of economic growth it is customary to attach more importance to the accumulation of physical capita. Now it is increasingly recognised that the growth of tangible capital stock depends to a considerable extent on human capital formation which is the process of increase of knowledge, the skills and capacity of all people of the country.

Bhutan from the very beginning of the planning era gave a high priority to the growth of education and literacy. Perhaps there are only few countries of the world like Bhutan that spent more than 10 per cent of their national expenditure on the growth of education in the early decades of planning. Bhutan started from a narrow base. In 1961 there were only 59 primary schools; there was not a single higher secondary school before this period. There was neither any technical school nor any degree college. Bhutan's important strategy of development after 1961 was to increase the number of primary schools, convert some of the schools into higher secondary and then to establish a college. (There is now one degree college in Bhutan). The pyramid of education structure was founded in Bhutan after 1961. In every plan, the number of schools, enrolment and investment on human resources increased. This is illustrated in Table - 1.

Table 1

Growth of Education in Bhutan

Period	*Investment (Lakh Ng)*	*Student Population*	*Percentage of plan allocation*
First Five Year Plan	94.95	9,190	8.21
Second Five Year Plan	357.07	11,610	17.61
Third Five Year Plan	900.00	16,571	19.00
Fourth Five Year Plan	1300.00	26,470	17.00

(Source : Prepared from the figures in *Druk Losel,* 1:1, May 1980, pp.5-7).

It is apparent from Table 1 that within 15 years the student population increased about three times. This is an important achievement because it is difficult to recruit teachers in Bhutan. More than 75 per cent of teachers are recruited form India.[15]

One of the novel features of the syllabi in the schools is that "agricultural farming" has been introduced as compulsory curricular activity in the schools. OXFAM had assisted to introduce the subject in all the schools of Bhutan.[16]

Adult education has been started by the Manpower Department at the Royal Commercial Institute, Thimpu. At Kalikhota, a similar adult education centre was started. Further a farmer's training programme is being organised at the sub-divisional level periodically. The training programme imparts various modern techniques of agricultural farming varying from scientific sowing to plant protection measures. A health school has been opened in the General Hospital of Thimpu. The health assistants are posted to various basic health units located in the rural areas of Bhutan. A medical school is being set up with the assistance of UNDP and UNIÇEF. A Royal Bhutan Polytechnique was started in Deothang and this technical school is an excellent example of international cooperation. The Teachers' Training Institute at Samchi has the objective of training the in-service teachers. Apart from all these new institutions, Bhutan arranges to send its students for higher training in India and Bangladesh.[17]

Bhutan has, however, concentrated to provide a broad-based general education. This has not debarred the importance of "rural flavour" in the curricula of all the schools. In a country whose resources are predominantly agricultural and pastoral, this strategy for man-power planning is very important step in the early stage of economic development.[18] Broadly speaking Bhutan's main strategy of development is to lay the foundation of future growth by investing in human resources. This strategy of economic development through the improvement of the quality of human resources at the shortest possible time is one of the new strategies adopted in this part of the region. This approach has been designated as a variety of basic need approach to development and growth.

Rural Development and Dualism

Not much information is available on the tenurial system of agriculture. However, land revenue system is considered to be feudalistic and it is also known that in large parts of Bhutan farmers practise "shifting cultivation".[19] Land reform measures started from 1952. At that time a ceiling was put on larger holdings to 30 acres and the "excess land" was distributed to the landless farmers. But the predominant strategy it appears from the scanty data that is available, is not to change the feudalistic pattern but to open new areas for farming. Bhutan has a vast uninhabitated territory. Many landless people have been settled in the new areas known as "settlement areas".[20] These settlement areas is part and parcel of the project known as "rehabilitation project". The scheme is mainly meant for the landless rural farmers. The scheme was started in Gaylephug which was uninhabited even in the early seventies. This is a unique experiment in human habitation. In this area, land was given to the landless according to the size of the family. These projects are the"planned villages" of Bhutan and are likely to be future granary for the country.[21]

Rehabilitation Project and Settlement Areas involve a transfer of population from one part to another. This has been achieved neither by force nor by coercion but by financial incentives.[22]

Rural reconstruction is intimately connected with the problem of rural credit. Till 1980, there was hardly any institution to help the rural farmers with easy access to credit. During the 46th National Assembly session members debated and passed a rural credit scheme. Three types of loans would be offered to the farmers. (i) Short-term loans should be given to meet the immediate needs of the farmers. The size of this loan will range from Nu 110 to Nu 1000 and carry an interest of 6 per cent. (ii) The second category would be medium-term loans and this would be offered for cleaning, fencing and terracing land, putting up subsidiary irrigation channels, purchasing cattle and seeds. The maximum limit for these loans will be Nu 3000. Loans under this category will carry an interest rate of 8 per cent. (iii) The third category of loans would be offered to buy machinery. The maximum amount of loan available in this category is 40 per cent of the total cost of machinery. These loans carry an interest of 10 per cent.[23]

In addition to the rural credit scheme a new type of loan is given to the farmers. At the 49th session of the National Assembly consumption loans to the farmers have been granted. Under this new scheme, loans will be paid upto the maximum Nu 1000 Nu, 2000 in case of house building, marriage, annual festivals and other family ceremonies. The Bank of Bhutan is responsible for implementing all the schemes connected with the farmers.[24]

Bhutan is trying her best to go away from the traditional system of farming to new cash crops. Bhutan is experimenting with sugar cane and potatoes. Orange and cardamom are the two principal cash crops of Bhutan at the moment. Bhutan is giving special attention to the production of cardamom. In order to assure a good price to the growers of cardamom, the Food Corporation of Bhutan is buying all the cardamom from the growers "keeping in view of the welfare of the public". The government fixes the price of cardamom at periodic intervals. Fixation of price of cardamom is a debated issue in Bhutan.[25] In case of oranges special methods have been undertaken to boost the production. Orange has become an important raw material for industrial development of Bhutan.

The major hurdle in the inaccessible area is the lack of water supply. Water schemes are being implemented in Bhutan. A number of rural water supply schemes (RWSS) has been completed in Samudrapjonkhar, Singhkherlouri and Diafam subdivisions apart from other accessible areas. At present 10 to 20 villages are covered in each year under RWSS.

It is difficult indeed to suggest the actual rate of growth of agricultural production in Bhutan. The growth in agricultural production seems to be less than 1 per cent per annum according to the World Bank Development Report of 1982. But the *Kuensel* in its supplementary number of 1979 put the rate of growth of agriculture at more than 1 per cent and near about 2 per cent. In any case the progress seems to be slow and Bhutan's present yield in 1977 as quoted in the Kuensel seems to be about 40 per cent lower than the Asia's average (which is 2458 kg per hectare for the cereals).[26] Hence, it is difficult to say whether any break-through has been affected in agriculture.

Apart from being an agricultural country Bhutan is also a pastoral country. A large section of people depend on sheep and yak breeding. Government is trying its best to change the old system of breeding by new methods. Two new sheep farms have been opened in the country, one in Bumthang and the other in Tashiyangphy. Weaving of woolen garments being the most important occupation of the people living in the Alpine region, the Government is trying to step up wool production with the help of some Colombo Plan countries. The Department of Animal Husbandry in consultation with UNDP, FAO has prepared a "Livestock Act and Bye Laws" for the country. The main purpose is to raise the nutritional standard and income of the people and in particular of those farmers who live mostly on the livestock products.[27]

It should be mentioned that in many parts of Bhutan "shifting cultivation" was practised. In the National Policy of 1974, the government has completely banned the "shifting cultivation." In order not to cause hardship to population dependent on this type of cultivation, it was decided that appropriate compensation would be paid to the displaced persons. Some were transferred to the settlement areas.

Bhutan, thus, is slowly emerging from the primitive system of cultivation to the modern system of farming. This, in Bhutan, has led to "dualistic" form of development. The co-existence may be attributed to the phenomenon of "technological dualism". Very often it appears in many developing society that the phenomenon of technological dualism not only persists but also grows because the relatively modern sector experiences an intensive application of modern scientific knowledge and technology to the process of production. Because of predominance of the backward sector the modern sector becomes an "enclaved system" restricted to high productivity activity at certain centres. The characteristics of enclaved modern sector generates a pattern of market-cum-technological relations whereby the backward sector remains subordinate to the modern sector in terms of serving the vested interest of the latter.

Whether this dualism will increase in Bhutan in the rural sector may be a matter of debate and conjecture. But this problem in Bhutan needs some special mention. The land tenure system in Bhutan, unless otherwise disproved, has still remained old, pre-feudal or feudal. A common feature of this system is to create a privileged class whose commitment to rural development is minimal. Comprehensive land reform programmes are talked about but are not introduced. In any society like Bhutan control of farmland remains a principal key to wealth, status and power. It is generally true that a few individuals or monasteries own large proportion of land and they dominate the local people through the varied roles as landlords, lenders and employers. Many farmers in Bhutan lack secure access to the basis of economic life—farm land. The incentive to production remains uncertain. Hence, the extent of the market is limited due to low purchasing power of the people. The production of industrial commodities and imports are coloured by the demand of the newly emerging elites. The landless, small or marginal farmers are too poor to create a market for industrial growth. The market for industrial production remains limited.

Industrial Growth in Bhutan : Birth of Private Capitalism

Since the market is limited and finance is difficult to get Bhutan has remained largely an agricultural—pastoral country. However, some attempts were made in the early part of the seventies to start some industries. To begin with, it was felt necessary to create an industrial estate in Phuntsholing so that all industries could be concentrated in one place, to avail of the common infrastructural facilities like power, water and transportation. The town is situated in the southern part of the country and is in the border of India. One of the important problems faced by industries in Bhutan is the absence of technical manpower. Almost all the skilled labourers have to be brought from India. This shortage of adequate manpower has slowed down the growth of industries in Bhutan which is mainly concentrated in Phutsholing. There are about 25 small scale units in the town which developed between 1972 and 1980.[28]

The small scale units in Bhutan are classified into two categories: (i) industries based on local resources and (ii) industries based on consumer demand. From 1980 Bhutan started to shift emphasis from small scale to larger industries. Pendent Cement Plant is the first large scale industry established under Indo-Bhutan co-operation. Further, at the initial stage of industrialisation (i.e. in the seventies) the policy was to concentrate in one particular area all the small units. But the recent policy is to disperse units nearer to the sources of raw materials for example, dolomite units of Pagli, Coal briquetting unit at Samudrapjonkhar, tile units at Dagpala, lime Kiln unit at Samchi, mustard oil expeller at Tashiang etc.[29]

With the modest beginning in industrialisation an important institutional structure has emerged in Bhutan. This is the birth of new entrepreneurship or the beginning of the private sector, however, rudimentory it might be. Private sector has started to appear in the seventies and at the initiative of His Majesty an Association of Private Sector Entrepreneurs has been formed on April 17, 1980.[30]

Entrepreneurs in the private sector can go for collaboration with its Indian counterpart only on issues strictly "technical". Financial or managerial collaboration with Indian private entrepreneurs is not encouraged. In other words, only technical know-how of the collaboration will be allowed to be brought in by the entrepreneurs. It was also clarified that technical collaboration proposals will be minutely examined by the Government and will be granted only to the deserving entrepreneurs on the basis of merit.[31]

The industrial policy measures as adopted by Bhutan have certain salient features:

(i) Private capitalism in Bhutan can develop only under state patronage.

(ii) Indian private capital is not encourged to come to dominate the industrial sector of Bhutan.

The second part of the policy prescription is in sharp contrast with Nepal's attitude to Indian private sector. In Nepal by and large Indian industrialists are not debarred from making direct investment. For example, the Indian industrialists inspired by the offer of liberal new Industrial Policy of 1981 in Nepal are operating in about 22 joint ventures with their Nepalese counterpart in the sphere of textiles, vehicles, engineering, food products, alcohol, hotelling, etc. The "joint ventures" as it is called in Nepal is another form of Indian private investment in Nepal and this type of investment is gradually gaining momentum in Nepal.[32] But in Nepal the Indian capitalists have gathered an "ugly image" by their acts of omissions and commissions. Perhaps the "ugly Indian" image of Indian capitalists, prominently displayed by public media, has prevented the Bhutan Government to go in for any joint venture with them. By and large, the Indian capitalists have earned a bad name in Nepal as well as in Bhutan.[33]

Bhutan's Dependence on India and Attempted Diversification

Bhutan's economic base is extremely poor. For planning and development Bhutan's own resources are not sufficient. "Out of every Nu 100 earned by people, the government levies only 12 to 15 chhetrums as tax, this by comparison is one of the lowest tax rates in the world. The rest of the funds have to be financed from external sources.[34]

In 1961 a Draft Five Year Plan for Bhutan was prepared by the Planning Commission of India and Government of India agreed to finance it entirely. The total outlay in the Plan was Rs. 1750/- lakhs. The Second Five Year Plan was launched in 1966 and it was entirely financed by India and the total outlay of the plan was about Rs. 2000/- lakhs. Bhutan made her own efforts to prepare the Draft Third Year Plan. Basically, the structure of the three plans is same. In all the plans emphasis was given on the development of infrastructure, like road, irrigation, social services and education. But a slight shift of emphasis was discerned in the Third Five Year Plan as Bhutan gave some attention to the development of small scale industries from this time. Again, unlike the previous plans, which were entirely financed by India, the Third Five Year Plan was partly financed by Bhutan's own resources. Out of total outlay of Rs. 3550 lakhs, the Indian Government contributed Rs. 3300 lakhs and Rs. 250 lakhs were from the resources of Bhutan.[35]

Bhutan's Fourth Five Year Plan was prepared by the Planning Commission of Bhutan. The outlay of the Plan is roughly six times bigger than that of the First Five Year Plan. The total contribution of India was nearly two times bigger than the Third Five Year Plan but the relative share of Indian assistance came down sharply. The Foreign Minister informed the Assembly that during the Fourth Five Year Plan "the country received assistance worth Nu 5271,000 from India and Nu 3260,000 from U.N. agencies and other countries." In terms of proportion, India's share in Bhutan's first two plans was 100 per cent and in the Fourth it was about 56 per cent. This means that India's importance in financing the plan has gradually declined over the period and the trend has continued in the subsequent plans. Bhutan's current thinking can be summarised from a resolution adopted in the 51st Session of the National Assembly: "It would not be proper to continuously depend on the assistance from India, as they themselves are badly constrained by over-population and frequent natural calamities. Should the situation ever rise where Government of India is in a position to provide only 50 per cent of the total assistance they are providing now, the financial situation of Bhutan will become critical. Of course, owing to the able leadership of His Majesty and the good fortune of the people, assistance could always be sought from other sources. However, Bhutan cannot rely on external assistance from all time to come. We cannot over rule the fact that our dependence on external assistance would prove detrimental to the sovereignty of the country.... The goal of Bhutan is self-reliance.[36]

Bhutan is receiving foreign aid mainly from two sources other than India, namely the U.N. agencies and the Colombo Plan countries. The main point to note is that Bhutan has alternative sources of getting loans other than India. Among the Colombo Plan countries Australia is the largest donor followed by the U.K. and Japan.[37]

Self-reliance for Bhutan is possible if her trade can expand. But exportable commodities in Bhutan are few in number. The main items exported are cardamom and timber. The major emphasis of Bhutan is to exploit the forest resources for export. But this strategy may be inconsistent with the goal of ecological balance in this sensitive part of the Himalayas.

Bhutan's forest represents its most valuable natural resources. The standing stock of timber is estimated at 500 million cubic meters and the potential annual cut is estimated at 2.5 million cubic metres. Thus far, commercially harvested timber have not exceeded 300,000 cubic metres a year, in part because of the lack of infrastructure and of modern felling equipment. Under the Fifth Five Year Plan considerable resources were allocated for the construction of forest roads and of ropeways and mechanisation of logging operations, and the annual volume of timber production is projected to increase fourfold by 1990. To increase the value added of forest based products the government maintains restrictions on the export of logs and sawn woods which account for 90 per cent of total timber exports. However, in spite of all attempts to increase the exports of timber Bhutan's balance of trade is in serious difficulties.[38]

Table 2

Bhutan's Balance of Payments (million U.S. Dollars)

	1979-80	*1980-81*	*1981-82*	*1982-83*
1. Exports f.ob	16.5	16.7	20.4	16.7
2. Imports c.i.f.	42.9	49.0	52.9	58.5
Exports as p.c. of Imports	38.46	34.08	39.50	28.54
3. Services and Private transfers (net)	-16.0	-18.0	-25.7	-29.5
4. Current balance	-42.4	-50.3	-57.7	-71.3

Source : I.M.F. Survey, February 20, 1984.

It is clear from the above table that Bhutan's balance of payments is in deficits and that there is a tendency of the deficits to increase over the period.

There is hardly any scope for Bhutan to bridge the gap between imports and exports. A key element in the government's industrialisation programme is the harnessing of the country's water resources for the generation of electricity. The Chukha Hydro Electricity Project, under construction since 1974, is the largest development project in Bhutan. The project's peak capacity is 336 megawatts. The project has been operational from the mid 1985. Since Bhutan's own needs absorb only a fraction of the output from the Chukha project, the bulk of the electricity is exported to India and part of revenue so derived will be used for servicing the loan for the project. Indian assistance for the project is estimated at about $ 200 million of which 60 per cent is in grants and 40 per cent in the form of loans, the loan is payable over 15 years period at 5 per cent interest. Government revenues from the Chukha project net of debt servicing and maintenance expenditure, are estimated at about Nu 100 million annually equivalent to the Government 's total receipts from all domestic sources in 1982-83. Earning from Chukha project will also help to reduce Bhutan's large deficits with India.

The domestic situation is given below to understand the seriousness of her problems arising out of paucity of resources.

Table 3

Central Government Budget of Bhutan (in million nqultrum)

	1979-80	*1980-81*	*1981-82*	*1982-83*
Receipts	307	321	408	476
(i) Tax Revenues	51	53	60	78
(ii) Non Tax Revenues	43	49	41	54
(iii) Foreign Grants	213	219	307	344
Foreign Grants				
As percentage of				
Receipts	69.38	68.22	75.24	72.27
Expenditure				
(i) Current	325	330	437	553
(ii) Capital	170	161	267	345
Overall Surplus/Deficits	–19	–9	–29	–77
As per cent of GDP	2.1	0.9	2.4	5.3

Computed from the I.M.F. Survey, Feb. 1984

It should be noted from Table -3 that *foreign grants are about 70 per cent of the total receipts of the Government of Bhutan*. This means that both current and capital expenditure are largely financed by the foreign grants.

Inflation has been a great problem of Bhutan. It is very often suggested that the rate of inflation in the urban areas has crossed the two-digit figures from the beginning of the 1980's. But no reliable data are available. However, the money supply in Bhutan has consistently increased. This is illustrated in the following Table 4.

Table 4

Money Supply in Bhutan in million nqulcrum

	1979-80	*1980-81*	*1981-82*	*1982-83*
Broad Money	155.0	202.1	239.5	275.7
Money Supply	102.7	121.5	137.5	147.7
Quasi Money	53.3	80.6	102.1	128.0

Source : I.M.F. Survey Feb. 1984.

Serious inflation has to a certain extent led the Bhutan Government to impose drastic price control on almost all the commodities in Bhutan. Price control has become an important feature of the Sixth Five Year Plan which started on January 1988. One of the reasons given is that "prices of some of the commodities rose by 300 to 400 per cent by the time those reached Jaigon to Thimpu."[39] The Government order proclaimed—"Business houses have been directed to sell commodities only at prices approved by the Department of Trade and Industries." The price control measures, however, are applicable only at the wholesale level and not on the retail level. It is a moot point, how far this measure will check the uncontrolled price in Bhutan. In fact, more the control the more powerful is the bureaucracy. After the development of planning, the bureaucracy has become extremely powerful in

Bhutan and it has led to concentration of power.[40]

Modernisation efforts of the past two decades have resulted in the concentration of functions and centralisation of responsibilities that would have remained in the domain of the village. A new class has emerged in Bhutan due to "contracts and contacts."

The Government of Bhutan has become concerned that this trend will undermine the traditional self-reliance of the people. Therefore decentralisation of the developmental effort has been assigned a key role in the overall development strategy of the Fifth and the Sixth Plans. About one-fourth of total expenditure in the plans will be devoted to projects that are prepared and implemented locally. With the exception of specialised inputs, local administration will make available construction materials for developmental projects in their region and arrange for "voluntary labour". Typical projects are irrigation facilities, livestock breeding and building of schools, health centres, feeder roads, suspension bridges and other small scale projects.[41]

Bhutan's Search for Identity : The SAARC Experiment

The virtues of trade expansion and integration among developing countries are no longer disputed in theory. At the government level, it is customary to pay tribute to the goals of cooperation and even integration of the third world countries. Since the last two decades, one can hardly count the occasions where governments of the third world would have solemnly proclaimed their intention to form regional or sub-regional common markets. SAARC proposal came as part of this search for regional co-operation.

It was at the invitation of the Government of Sri Lanka seven[42] South Asian countries viz. Bangladesh, Bhutan, India, Maldives, Nepal, Pakistan and Sri Lanka met in Colombo for the first time from 21st April to 23rd April,1981 to consider the Bangladeshi proposal as outlined in the working paper. Bhutan enthusiastically joined the movement. The ground rules for negotiation was that "decisions should be taken on the basis of unanimity" and "bilateral and contentions issues were to be excluded from this deliberations".[43]

The Foreign Secretaries further agreed that 'regional cooperation was not intended or expected to be a substitute for bilateral and multilateral cooperation but could complement both; nor should it be consistent with bilateral and multilateral obligations".[44] In this way, by keeping controversial and unresolved bilateral issues out of the picture and by looking upon SAARC as complementary to existing areas of bilateral and multilateral cooperation, a basis as well as a search for maximum convergence of interests was possible. Bhutan's approach as to the scope for regional cooperation appears to be similar to that of Bangladesh. While refraining from using any reference to political and security objectives, it lays stress on expanding cooperation in the cultural, infrastructural, scientific and technological fields as also in relation to global negotiation with the developed countries.

In the second meeting of the SAARC, the need for an institutional agreement was reiterated by the Bangladesh Foreign Secretary. He pointed out that "without any institutional mechanism, regional co-operation would be relegated to the realm of ideal.'[45] Bangladesh was supported by Nepal, Sri Lanka and Bhutan. Bhutan supported the demand for "institutionalisation". "The countries in other regions of the world who had co-operated bilaterally and internationally with each other, had found it to be in their greater collective and individual interest to have an additional institutional framework for regional co-operation."

Pakistan made it clear that the establishment of an institutional framework was not feasible in the present circumstances. Such a framework should await development of greater regional understanding and complementarity in the economic of the regional economies. India's attitude towards institutionalisation of regional co-operation converged with that of Pakistan. India sounded a note of caution and pointed out that "institutionalisation" was pre-mature and should come only slowly and gradually.

The SAARC was originally conceived by Bangladesh and not India. Perhaps through SAARC the relatively smaller countries want to make their voices felt. Taken individually, Bhutan, Nepal, Bangladesh, Maldives or Sri Lanka may be weak but collectively they may pose a serious challenge to the big country, India. In the South East Asia, it seems that the smaller countries can make themselves felt by collective action.[46]

There are at least four difficulties in the direct pursuit of regional economic cooperation in this part of South Asia.[47]

First, India is so large in its size and potential and others relatively so small that any serious talk of trade and economic negotiations creates a fear psychosis. Population wise India is bigger than Bhutan by 518 times, Nepal by 46.1, Sri Lanka 46.7, Pakistan 8.2 and Bangladesh 7.6 times (approximately).

Second, countries come together in association if they have or feel to have a shared interest. India and Pakistan have common history but they do not have perception of shared interest.

Third, India has fallen into contradiction of her own creation. On the one hand, she speaks about regional co-operation and on the other insists on bilateralism as determined by strategic considerations. India cannot pursue the apparently contradictory paths at the same time to face her neighbours.

Fourth, where the economic benefits are obvious there would be a strong pull for cooperation. At present, the total intra-regional trade is about 2 billion dollars as against the total regional exports of 28 to 30 billion dollars.

The question whether the economics of the SAARC countries are complementary or competitive[48] should also not be given undue importance. The example of the EEC countries forcefully tells us that the process of development itself creates new complementarity as well as competitiveness. The EEC countries were very competitive when the era of cooperation began but through cooperation and development, they created a vast area of complimentarities.

Bangladesh, Nepal and Bhutan might have initially entertained the hope of exercising greater leverage with their more dominant partner—India, in respect of several unsettled contentious bilateral issues. India, however, anticipating such a move from the smaller states, made it quite explicit prior to the meeting of Foreign Secretaries that such issues could have no place in this regional forum. A clause in the Joint Communique issued at the end of the First meeting made this quite clear in no uncertain terms.[49]

Smaller states like Bhutan, are however anxious to accelerate the pace of SAARC. Herein may lie the danger of India. The early politicisation of the forum as well as the launching of ambitious projects requiring huge funding will inevitably bring in the influence of major powers in the region. It is then the real test of SAARC as well as India will begin.

Relationship between a small state like Bhutan and a large state like India is bound to be a complex one. Bhutan, through SAARC or similar organisations may try to break the hold of bilaterialism in its relation with India. This has been clearly demonstrated recently in negotiations between India and Bhutan regarding the financing of the current Sixth Five Year Plan of Bhutan. Similarly, other powers may be brought into increase the options of Bhutan. Bhutan may be interested in maximising her options in trade and aid, considering the limitations of her domestic resources.

Summary and Conclusion

It is difficult to come to any "conclusion" regarding Bhutan because of the paucity of basic data and due to lack of any accepted criterion for judging the success and failure of developmental efforts of a country which has a large better sector, an important pastoral economy and a primitive agriculture. The 'jhum' or shifting cultivation was widely prevalent a few decades back in various parts of Bhutan. There was hardly any monetary or financial institution of modern type even three decades back; there was hardly any scientific census upto the period of January 1988, when the first official census went into operation; there was no college or technical institution two decades before. Nearly seventy per cent of the kingdom is under forest; railways are non-existent; electricity came to Bhutan only in 1962; there are only 414 km of paved road as late as 1980. Centuries of self-imposed isolation of people from the rest of the world has led them to cultural, ideological and social seclusion. The system of administration is monarchical. The country's Chief Administrative Body is the 12-member Royal Advisory Council. Most of the members of the Royal Advisory Council are drawn from the Civil Services and the Buddhist hierarchy, except the four ministers who are appointed by the king himself. For administrative purposes the country is divided into four regions - East, Central, West and South—each administered by a Governor appointed by King; Dzongdas (Commissioners) maintain law and order in the 16 districts (Dzongs). The villages are administered by the headman elected under one-family-one-vote system.

There are many models of development differing in priorities and strategies. There cannot be universal model for development; each country has to choose its development style suited to its socio-cultural realities, its endowment of natural resources, the genius and skills of people and its vision of good life. Bhutan is a late starter in development process and from the beginning Bhutan gave emphasis on the development of infrastructure, quality of human resources and rural upliftment. It is in this sense Bhutan's model of development is a "variation" of the "basic-need" approach to growth.

An approach that concentrated on meeting the basic needs emphasises improvements in health, nutrition and basic education —especially through improved and redirected public services, such as rural water supplies, sanitation facilities, and primary schools. It has been argued that direct provision of such goods and services affects poverty more immediately than those approaches that rely on raising income and productivity of the poor.[50] The critical question for a country like Bhutan is : will the provision of basic goods and services slow down a country's growth rate? In other words, is there a trade-off between growth of the GDP and basic needs? From a theoretical standpoint there may be no necessary reason for such trade off; but the evidence is not conclusive. Countries which have emphasised basic needs such as Burma and Tanzania may be seen to have done so at the cost of lower growth rates of output.[51] This issue is raised in the context of Bhutan in view of the data given by the World Bank which shows that Bhutan experienced a very low rate of growth of the GDP (about 0.2 per cent) during 1972-1981 period. This issue is complicated by many factors which effect growth other than the elements emphasised in theory; that is allocation of resources between social services and other productive sectors. The true impact of a planned programme oriented towards basic needs thus becomes very difficult to evaluate.

In spite of the basic need approach certain questions emerge from Bhutanese strategy for development. Why has it been so difficult for public programmes to have a development effect on the Bhutanese poor to date? Central Government of Bhutan operates at a severe disadvantage when they try to move public goods and services down to the local level to benefit the weakest of the community. The first of these advantages is the Bhutanese system of administration often does not reach effectively below the district or zonal level. When it does, it is usually done in a single point fashion such as the introduction of a new seed variety, a new road, a visit by the public health worker etc. Public inputs are frequently made without much knowledge of or concern for the local resources base. Instructions originate from those farthest removed from the field and flow with little or no modification enroute. In the interests of uniformity in operations and speed of implementation, little thought is given how to tailor programme to local needs and conditions.

When it does reach directly to the local level, the central government frequently works through intermediate agencies, such as village chieftain or headman or local landlords that provide services to the assetless poor. The idea is that local people will make use of these intermediate agencies to obtain the specific, technically defined and allocated goods and services of the government. A major difficulty of this approach is that all local people do not have equal opportunity to use intermediaries either directly or through groups. On the contrary, what we see happening is that local elites who possess assets or some political power (often both) gaining preferential access to these public inputs and thus consuming the lion's share of public good and services alloted to the rural sector. Can such limited forms of participation produce structural changes in the circumstances and capabilities of the rural poor? With top-down approaches which allow little or no room for effective participation in decision making, evaluation and project control, can people ever develop the skills and political voice to decide and manage their destiny? Can their development come about?

The questions like these are likely to remain in some dispute especially in the context of Bhutan when after nearly three decades of planning, Bhutan is seriously thinking of giving some emphasis on decentralisation of power. We note, without claiming that the argument is conclusive, that some kind of alternative approaches are warranted if one is serious about wanting to reach the most disadvantaged rural people in Bhutan. Bhutan is listed as one of the 'least developed countries' of the world.

The centre-periphery relationship has become a very stable subject due to its constant repetition. But in the context of Bhutan this centre-periphery economic relationship has some relevance and importance. As is obvious modernisation process in Bhutan came into existence partly in response to cumulated exogenous developments and partly due to (what is called) "trade-need-based-technoloigical-use".[52] So "modernisation remains confined to certain areas of production belonging to certain administrative and commercial centres." In this way, enclaved growth centres emerged which were completely external to periphery. The process of expansion has led to creation of two extremes—enclaved growth centres and under development at the periphery. However, the "enclaved growth centres" can act as catalyst agents for development in Bhutan. In the "modernised" sector such potential catalyst agents surely do exist in Bhutan; and such catalyst agents convey a philosophy of planned change which goes beyond the single sector programme and it involves a commitment to increase productivity, equality and self-reliant decision making, but they have not yet been identified. Private capitalism has just appeared in Bhutan under the state patronage and protection. Very often this emergence is related to the existing feudal structure, and the tiny industrial sector is too insignificant to make any radical or effective change.

Bhutan's relationship with India is complex. India is the largest donor for Bhutan's planned development. India's technical and financial help in all the sectors are substantial. But Bhutan, like many other states, feel that to put all eggs in one basket may create a relationship which may go against the declared principle of self-reliance and self-esteem. Bhutan is apparently trying to diversify her sources of loan, aid and technical help. This diversification process started form the mid-seventies. Bhutan is searching for an "identity". In this search India should see an improvement of regional (or even global) economic scenario. Whether the issue is aid, grant or trade, countless opportunities arise for friction and policy disagreement. The costs of not resolving these types of differences between the two neighbouring countries within a common framework are too high to ignore. Foreign relations are like human relations. They are endless. The solution of one problem usually leads to another. However, there is no basic contradiction between India and Bhutan. Progress is not created by contended people. An idealist believes the shortrun does not count; a cynic believes that the long run does not matter. A realist believes that what is done or left undone in the short run determines the long run.

References

1. Bikram Jit Hasrat—*History of Bhutan - Land of Peaceful* Dragon, (Bhutan, Education Department, 1979), p. 1-10.

2. Dilip Bhattacharyya—Bhutan—The Himalayan Paradise: (Oxford and IBH Publishing, 1975), p. 12.

3. I.M.F. (a) *Survey*, (February 20, 1984), p. 50. (b) Bhutan's population figures can be found in Asian Business Directory BT (1) (Kothari and Sons, Confederation of Asian Chamber of Commerce, 1976). (c) Bhutan did not have any regular Census till 1988. *The Kuensel* (Jan 23, 1988) writes "The Census of Thimpu begins soon and Census will be the first Official Census covering Thimpu, Dechencholling Simtokha, Motithang and Yanchenphung".

4. Description of these "clusters" could be found in *Himalayan Traders* by Christopher von Furer Haimendorf (John Murray, 1975), pp. 24-60.

5. *Kuensel*, (February 1977), p. 2.

6. *Kuensel—Supplementary*, (Nov. 15-29,1979), p. 4.

7. Social and economic systems of Bhutan remained static for centuries. Polyandry and polygamy are still prevalent in many parts. In a recent debate on polyandry some letters were published in the *Kuensel* (1987-88) about the utility or otherwise of the system of Bhutan's economy.

8. *I.M.F. Survey* (Feb. 20, 1984), p. 50.

9. *I.M.F. Survey* (July 16, 1982), p. 185.

10. World Bank Development Report, 1981 quoted by I.N. Mukherjee in "South Asian Regional Cooperation: An Evaluation of Attitudes and Perceptions of Constituent States" in *South Asia* ed. by Agwani, Roy, Kumar, Mukherjee and Muni, (Chandigarh, CRRID, 1983), p. 8.

11. Nirmal Das—"Nepalese Migration to India—Search for an Identity" in *Man and Development*, Vol. IV, (Chandigarh, CRRID,March 1982), pp. 167-168.

12. See, Nirmal Das—*The Nepalese of North East India and their Politics* (M. Phil Dissertation, J.N.U., New Delhi 1981). p. 169.

13. *Kuensel* (Feb. 1, 1977)

14. Hasrat, *op.cit.*

15. "75 per cent of teachers are from India" *Kuensel*, Vol. XII No. 1 (Jan. 2, 1977), p. 3.

16. *Kuensel*, Vol. XI No. 19 (May 19, 1981), p. 1.

17. *Kuensel*, Vol. XVI No. 36 (Sept. 6, 1981), p. 2.

18. M. Das Gutpa—"Human Resources in Development in Bhutan" in *Novum Orcanum*, Vol. 5 No. 2 (Dec. 1985), pp. 1-8.

19. George Bogle observed in 1775 that people of Bhutan "may properly be divided into three classes : the priests, the servants or officers of the government and the landholders and the husbandmen" quoted by A. Deb in *Bhutan and India* (Calcutta, Firma K.L.M., 1976), p. 32. In Bhutanese rural economy peasantry was mostly consisted of *Khaips*. In fact these *Khaips* own land and are considered the most important *segement* of the population.

20. *Kuensel* - Vol. XI No. 49 (Dec. 5, 1976), p. 3.

21. (a) *Kuensel - Supplementary* (July 22, 1979), P. 4.

    (b) "Allotment of land to the landless at Chirag was carried out of 315 landless (Sukumbasis) and 150 had already been settled" *Kuensel*, Vol. XVI No. 9 (March 1981), p. 3.

22. *Kuensel Supplementary* (Nov. 15-29, 1979), p. 4.

23. *Kuensel Supplementary* (July 22, 1979), p. 4.

24. *Kuensel Supplementary* (Nov. 15, 1979), p. 2.

25. *Kuensel*, Vol XV No. 4 (Oct. 5, 1980), p. 2. See also "Report on Internal Market Survey of Large Cardamon" by Cardamom Board, Cochin, India, pp. 32-34 and 42. "80 per cent of the production of Bhutan is coming to Siliguri and re-booked to principal markets in India" p. 44

26. World Development Report (1982) (i) *Kuensel Suppl.* (Feb. 7, 1979 and Nov. 1979) (ii) *Druk Losel* commented in Vol. 2 No. 2, p. 26 "As a result of rapid change in agriculture, the income of the individual has increased from Nu 40 to Nu 400 within a span of 10 years."

27. *Kuensel* Vol. XV No. 4, (Oct. 5, 1980), p. 2.

28. *Kuensel* Vol. XV No. 12, (March 23, 1980), p. 1.

29. *Kuensel* Vol. XII No. 19 (April 25), p. 1-2.

30. *Kuensel* Vol XV (April 28, 1980).

31. *Kuensel* Vol. XV (Sept. 14, 1980).

32. (i) M.D. Dharmadasani—*India's Aid to Nepal, Nature and Quantum* (Occasional Paper Series 6, Centre For the Study of Nepal, B.H.U.

1982), p. 14.

(ii) M.P. Lama—*Economices* of Indo-Nepalese Co-operation, (New Delhi, M.N. Publishers, 1985), p. 111-121.

(iii) P. *Blaikie,* J. Cameron and D. Seddon—*Nepal in Crisis Growth and Stagnation at the Periphery* (Oxford University Press, 1983), pp. 79-84.

33. *Kuensel* Vol. XVI (Jan. 18, 1981).

34. (a) *Kuensel* Vol XVI (Jan. 18, 1981).

(b) *Kuensel* Vol. XV No. 16 (April 20, 1980)

(c) One Chhetrun is equivalent to one paise of Indian rupee and Nu 100 is nearly equivalent to Rs. 100.

35. M. Das Gupta—"Economic Development of Bhutan" in *Commerce* (Annual Number 1981), p. 240.

36. *Kuensel Supplementary* 52 Session of the Assembly, p. 2.

37. *I.M.F. Survey* (Feb. 20, 1984).

38. *Ibid.*

39. (a) *Kuensel* (January 30, 1988).

(b) Jaigaon is the border town of India near Bhutan.

40. Bhutan Government is keen to decentralise the power. For detail see, *Kuensel* Vol. XVI No. 20, (May 19, 1981).

41. What is the nature of growth in Bhutan? "During the Fifth FYP Bhutan's compound growth was 6.3 per cent but growth in real terms would be substantially lower. The fastest growing sector were forestry and logging (19 per cent), mining (20 per cent) and electricity (105 Per cent) (Kuensel) Jan 30, 1988 p. 3.

42. Having explained the need for regional co-operation with adequate safeguards the Working Paper identified eleven possible areas of co-operation.

43. Mukherjee, *op.cit.*

44. Joint Communique First Meeting of Foreign Secretaries, Colombo, April 23, 1981.

45. Mukherjee, *op.cit.* In May 1980, *Dawn,* a Pakistani paper editorially commented: "If the Bangladesh idea is for anything other than informal forum for consultation and if moves are to be made to institutionalise and

formalise this arrangement, it is certain to run into snags."

46. T.P. Bhatt—"Co-operation for Economic Development" in *South Asia*, pp. 35-49.

47. Sethi—"extended Regional Cooperation" in *South Asia, op.cit.*, pp. 50-51.

48. There are many important differences among the SAARC countries. For detail, see Bhatt, *op.cit.*

49. B. Satyanarayan—"The Prospects For Regional Economic Cooperation in South Asia "Paper presented at the All India Seminar on *South Asia* held under the auspices of Research in Rural and Industrial Development, (Chandigarh 2-5, January 1983).

50. See, Paul Streeten, "From Growth to Basic Need," in *Finance and Development*, (Sept. 1979).

51. See, Norman Hicks, "Growth vs. Basic Needs", in *World Development*, Vol. 7, (Nov.-Dec. 1979).

52. Alvi Hazna, : "Peripheral Capitalism" in *State and Society*, (April-June, 1981).

7

Economic Development of Bhutan : Problems and Strategies

B.P. MISRA

The purpose of this paper is to try to understand the problems and strategies of economic development in Bhutan. One strikingly important fact about the development plans in Bhutan is that they were sponsored and underwritten by the Government of India. This was done, undoubtedly, at the behest of the Government of Bhutan. Therefore, the development plans were a joint response to problems perceived by both the Governments. Another significant point to be noted is that the Government of Bhutan inaugurated its development programme and established its Development Department on as late as July 1, 1961. To understand the problems and strategies of development in Bhutan the timing of the plan needs closer examination.

An analysis of development process is always instructive.

But it becomes doubly meaningful and relevant when development is a conscious effort and is a part of social engineering. The quantum and direction of development must have an explanation in such a situation. A strategy of development is only another name for such an explanation.

However a study of strategy of development may as well end up being normative for precisely the same reason that development is deliberate. But the utility of such normative exercise will vary in direct relation with the validity of the explanatory framework.

As far as problems are concerned they may be visualised at two levels. In fact, a strategy is worked out because there are problems that need solution. Such initial problems may disappear once the action plan drawn according to the strategy is in progress. But there may be consequential or second-order problems arising out of plan implementation which may necessitate improvisation or complete overhaul of the strategy drawn at the first instance. An exercise into the problems and strategies of development in Bhutan should therefore endeavour to focus attention on both— the principal or primary problems/strategies and the secondary or derived problems and strategies.

In short, what is essential is to see through the development plans rather than providing a descriptive account of the same. An exception to this may be made only in those ideal cases where the people expected to benefit out of a plan are directly responsible for framing the same.

But the case of Bhutan otherwise. A hereditary monarchy since 1907, Bhutan is lacking in those institutions which characterise an open democratic society even though some experiments in that direction have been made since 1953, the year the *Tshogdu* (National Assembly) was established. It has been said "The few reports available on the Tshogdu electoral process indicate that constituency election meetings are dominated by the officials and traditional leaders. The consensus on a candidate, if one is reached, is thus a very narrow one among a small body of men, most of whom hold some official rank".[1] It has also been remarked "in a largely non-politicised society such as Bhutan where lines of authority are still functional and respected, a consensus at the top probably broadly reflects a consensus throughout the society, even at the local or district level.[2] Be that as it may, what is significant is the suggestion that the consensus at the top is what matters most. It is, therefore, necessary to understand the nature of perception of problems at the top to comprehend the strategy of development in Bhutan. It is also necessary to have a fair idea of what the economy of Bhutan was like before planning became a formal affair so that the character and pace of development during the plan-period may be better appreciated.

Socio-economic Condition of Bhutan before Plan Period

Although it is difficult to reconstruct what the economy of Bhutan was like in those days due to extreme paucity of data, it is worthwhile to piece together scattered information to have a broad overview of the same.

There was no vehicular traffic nor any motorable road to Bhutan then. From India one had to approach Bhutan through Sikkim via the Nathu La pass touching Yatung in Tibet on the way. Travel was done by foot, horse and yak. There were foot-tracks leading to Bhutan through the several Dooars but they were used sparingly because of difficult terrain. Also, "there were no telephones, electricity or sanitary fittings in those days... Most people managed well enough with the old-fashioned hurricane lantern, while the up-and-coming were taking, though rather hesitantly, to the dazzling splendour of the petromax pressure-lamp."[3]

The king took a direct and personal interest in the administration and had no statutory Chief Adviser or Chief Minister. Even the codification and reformation of the laws of Bhutan was personally handled by the king himself.[4] Only foreign relations and external trade were looked after by the Dorji family, the Head of which acted as the Bhutan Agent based in Kalimpong. The two families were related to each other and moreover, in 1952, King Jigme Dorji Wangchuk had married the Bhutan Agent Jigmie Dorji's younger sister. In fact most high officials were related to the king himself. In 1955, for example, the three Dzongpons (District Magistrates) of Byakar, Lhuntse and Shamgang were all relatives of the king.[5] In the same year, king's sister-in-law was appointed as Dzongpon at Tashigang in eastern Bhutan.[6]

In 1907, when dynastic rule was established in Bhutan, the Penlop (Governor) at Paro was hostile to it and even in later years he seemed never completely reconciled to playing second fiddle. "It is not a matter of surprise that the late Maharaja should have thought fit, in the early years of the dynasty, to retain power in his own hands and to appoint to posts of responsibility his own relatives on whom he could depend more fully for their loyalty."[7] Even as late as in 1955, it was said that the weight of the Central authority is felt more sensibly in the areas of central Bhutan, the ancestral home of the king, than in areas of western Bhutan, where the late Paro Penlop weilded a not inconsiderable influence.[8] It may be of some use to put on record here that during the Younghusband expedition to Tibet in 1904, the Wangchuks and Dorjis had sided with the British Government of India and collaborated with it while the Paro Penlop had been hostile to the same because of his leaning towards China

In Bhutan, holders of the highest offices engaged in trade.[9] The nineteenth century records testify that the Dharma and Deb Rajas of Bhutan were themselves the biggest traders.[10] A few years before the Plans began it was reported that some of the most respected monasteries were maintained on the proceeds of trade transactions, and high lamas were often most adept and shrewd in the conduct of commerce. King Jigmie Dorji Wangchuk's mother had a religious bent of mind, but her special interest was in weaving. She had a team of weaving-girls deployed throughout Bhutan, distributed yarn to them from a central headquarters at Thimphu, and bought it back as cloth of variegated Bhutanese designs, for sale both inside and outside Bhutan.[11] A favourite lady of the king was also a trader and she considered herself entitled to the free use of official transport for purposes of her private trade.[12] In 1955, it was reported that Dzongstap (Deputy Magistrate) at Paro understood and spoke Hindi obviously because "he has travelled fairly widely in India, both on pilgrimage and for trade."[13] The few illustrative cases that can be thus extracted also include the younger brother of the Bhutan Agent who "had always been more interested in trade."[14]

Until 1958, Bhutan's principal trade ties were with Tibet. Each important commercial centre in Bhutan had its own route across the Himalayan frontier. For example, Paro's trade followed a low pass which allows easy transit to Phari in Tibet. The merchants of Punakha travelled up the valley of the Mo Chu on their journey to Gyantse and Shigatse. One of the most frequent routes, through Laitsawa, was controlled by the merchants of Bhumthang for going up to Lhasa. Much of the trade between eastern Bhutan and Tibet followed the Lhobrak and Dozam rivers or crossed the eastern frontier into Tawang in Arunachal Pradesh from where an easy route led into Tibet. In addition to rice, Bhutan's chief exports to Tibet consisted of fine silk fabrics, vegetable dyes and brass utensils. Bhutan's chief imports from Tibet were salt, wool and precious metals.[15]

It was reported in 1955 that there were extensive private estates, mostly belonging to the close relatives of the king in central and eastern Bhutan. The tenants paid tribute in kind to their landlords.[16] The administration of the southern districts of Bhutan was entrusted with the Bhutan Agent at Kalimpong who was responsible for paying in a fixed amount annually to the Central exchequer, with no questions asked as to how much was actually realised form the people. He received no regular salary and was expected to maintain himself out of the proceeds of his charge. He also owned extensive private land in Bhutan itself.[17] The landed interests were generally apprehensive of any reform in land settlement for they might be asked to pay taxes in cash. Another fear was the possible hike in land-tax consequent upon the land reforms. The main difficulty in the way of tax reform came from Bumthang area, where about three-quarters of the cultivable

There were some problems regarding national integration in Bhutan. The Nepalese settled in western and southern Bhutan harboured resentment against the government for not being permitted to settle in the interior regions. The Government was considering giving full rights to the existing Nepalese in the State while providing adequate safeguards against all future immigration.[30] There were many Tibetan settlers as well, particularly in Wangdi Chholing area, who were mostly traders. They appeared to get along quite peacefully with the local Bhutanese but there was very little inter-action between the two communities. The Bhutanese showed a feeling of almost contempt towards the Tibetans whom they regarded as "a cowardly race who, time and again during their history, had been overrun and conquered by the Chinese."[31]

Indo-Bhutan Relations

However, such subjective attitudes should not be taken too seriously and out of context. The rulers of Bhutan had endeavoured in the past to keep Bhutan isolated lest it loses its independence. Unlike Tibet they were largely successful in this because of various extraneous reasons. But, after India became free in 1947 and began persuing its policy of integrating the princely states into Indian Union, Bhutan began feeling uneasy about its own prospect. At this stage, Bhutan thought of forging a federation with Sikkim in association with Nepal and Tibet as a counter-weight to India. But, nothing came of this. In late 1948 the King of Bhutan sent a delegation to India to sort out the scope of further relations. The Government of India assured the Government of Bhutan that it would respect Bhutan's autonomy if it maintained the same relationship with post-British India as it had maintained with British India.[32]

In 1949, a treaty between India and Bhutan was executed on the model of 1910 treaty, which stated, *inter alia*, that the Government of Bhutan agrees to be guided by the advice of the Government of

India in regard to its external relations. In the same year China became Communist and Mao Tse Tung declared that his Republic would wage the war of liberation to the very end and would liberate all the territories of China.[33] Soon after this China sent its liberation army to Tibet and established its control over the affairs there in 1950. Although India conceded the Chinese claim of suzerainty over Tibet, apprehensions were raised by many even in the official circles about the possible Chinese design on India's northern borders. There is no hard evidence that Peking considers Bhutan to be part of the great Chinese motherland but in the past, in the 1910-12 period, Peking had asserted its suzerainty over Bhutan in its correspondence with the British. Even though China has allowed this assertion to lapse, the claim by China on some parts of Bhutan in its published maps has helped the apprehension to be kept alive. In a statement to Parliament on December 6, 1950, Nehru declared : "From time immemorial the Himalayas have provided us with magnificent frontiers... We cannot allow that barrier to be penetrated because it is also the principal barrier to India.'[34]

It should be noted here that the conduct of India's relation with Bhutan was the responsibility of the Political Officer in Sikkim, who maintained contact with the kingdom through the Agent to the Bhutan Government, who had his head-quarters at Kalimpong. Nari Rustomji, an I.C.S. officer who was loaned to Sikkim as its Dewan (Prime Minister) during 1954-59, has the following to say about the relation that existed between the Political Officer and the Government of Bhutan:

"A convention had been established that every new incumbent to the office of Political Officer should call on the King to present his credentials. But even this courtesy call was generally arranged to take place not at Bhutan's capital, Thimpu but at Paro, some distance away. If the King and the Political Officer happened to hit it off, the King might invite the Political Officer to visit the capital and tour the country. It was rarely that a really close relationship developed between the King and the Political Officer, with the result, doubtless intended by Bhutan, that the country was left very much to its own devices, neither interfering with nor interfered with by the outside world."[35]

Rustomji had a deep personal friendship with Jigmie Dorji, Bhutan's Agent at Kalimpong, and his testimony of the state of affairs in those years, therefore needs closer scrutiny. Rustomji wrote:

> For India, Bhutan stood out as a wide gaping vacuum on frontier of vital strategic importance. The country was devoid of communications, and, should an emergency have necessitated the sending of troops, at Bhutan's request,for protection against an aggressor, sheer ignorance of the country alone would have stood in the way of effective action. The Government of India felt the time had come for strengthening India's ties with Bhutan... Jigmie agreed with the Government of India that Bhutan must move with the times, but had also his young King to convince. I had met the King only once, during his brief visit to Shillong, and we had not had the opportunity of getting to know each other closely. Jigmie hoped that, if we could see built up and there might be some rethinking in the King's mind regarding the whole question of opening up his country with India's assistance.[36]

Jigmie Dorji was hopeful that the renewal of acquaintance between the King and Rustomji might help in removing of suspicions and apprehensions about Bhutan taking aid from India for the economic development of the country. But, after his visit to Bhutan, Rustomji wrote:

> My impression is that while the Bhutan authorities would welcome aid for the implementation of their development projects, they are apprehensive of the implications and are reluctant to embark on any step that might have the effect of rendering them dependent on or under a sense of obligation to any external power.[37]

Rustomji also wrote:

> I do not claim to have made much contribution by way of advice on technical subjects such as agriculture or poultry. The King and his ministers knew more about such matters than I could teach them in a lifetime. My contribution was in the direction of highlighting the need for quickly training up a nucleus of young Bhutanese officers to act as the spearhead for the country's development."[38]

Rustomji also succeeded in obtaining the King's agreement to an extensive programme of road development,[39] but nothing came of this until a few years later.

Meanwhile, the extensive trade between Bhutan and Tibet was under stress. As has been said previously, rice was regularly exported form Bhutan to Tibet and salt imported from Tibet into Bhutan by way of exchange. An order was issued in early 1955 banning the export of rice from eastern Bhutan, the grounds being that it was required to meet internal demands. The Tibetans retaliated by banning the export of salt to Bhutan. This created something of a crisis, for it was found that, in the absence of easy transport, salt would cost the people nearly Rs. 40 per maund it transported into the interior from India. The Bhutanese Government's ban on rice export however originated form consideration other than of merely local demand. In the Bhutanese view, the Government of Tibet were not playing fair in the matter of Bhutanese trade. Bhutanese traders were permitted to take their goods only to certain prescribed marts in Tibet, where the greater portion had to be sold at Tibetan Government depots much below the normal market rates. The Bhutan Government's act was directed to breaking this practice of unfair restrictions not conducive to private trade.[39]

In 1955, Jigmie Dorji had also arranged for R.K. Nehru, India's Foreign Secretary, to visit Bhutan and meet the King.[40] It appears from subsequent records that consequent upon the visit by Nari Rustomji and R.K. Nehru, Bhutan had agreed to receive

India's offer of gifts on a very small scale. In 1956, Bhutan accepted 146 tons of fertilizers, 2000 maunds of cement and hospital equipment worth about Rs. 2.6 lakhs. She also accepted some scholarships for Bhutanese students to study in India. During 1956-57, Bhutan received financial assistance from India amounting to Rs. 3.22 lakhs. The total Indian aid to Bhutan for similar reasons during the year 1957-58 stood at Rs. 2.45 lakhs.[41]

In September 1958, Jawaharlal Nehru visited Bhutan, "The highlight of the visit was mammoth public meeting where perhaps for the first time in Bhutan's history, some thousands of villagers were gathered to hear of the future of their country, of India's friendship for Bhutan, of the dark clouds that threatened from the north."[42]

Nehru strongly urged the Royal Government to modify its isolation policy, at least to the extent of accepting Indian economic aid. New Delhi was particularly interested in the construction of a road connecting India with central and western Bhutan which would have obvious strategic and economic significance.

Bhutan's immediate response was non-committal despite its own increasing concern over happenings in the north. When Nehru was asked how Bhutan had reacted to India's offer of aid, he replied : "you will be surprised to learn how reluctant the Maharaja is. He is not at all happy. He could have had aid the last two or three years if he had asked for it."[43]

But within a short span of six months, the situation changed dramatically. In March 1959 a massive uprising against the Chinese in Lhasa was finally suppressed. The Dalai Lama made his escape to India through Tawang in Arunachal.

The Government of Bhutan wanted to stop the Tibetan refugees who had started fleeing Tibet from entering Bhutan. As has been pointed out earlier, due to historical reasons, the Bhutanese have no great liking for the Tibetans. Apart from that, the Bhutanese Government was not inclined to admit Tibetans for fear of Bhutan earning the wrath of China. The Bhutanese soldiers were also afraid of the Khampas making their way down, for, they were terrified of being looted if the Khampas did come.[44]

Bhutan had been administering eight enclaves in Western Tibet since the seventeenth century. China seized them in the summer of 1959.[45] At about the same time the Government of Bhutan decided to withdraw its representative from Lhasa and its officers from western Tibet and close its borders with Tibet.[46] Nehru stated in the Indian Parliament on 23rd August 1959 that the protection of the borders and the territorial integrity of Bhutan was the responsibility of India and that India would consider any aggression on Bhutan as an aggression on India.[47]

On 18th September 1959 a delegation led by Jigmie Dorji visited New Delhi to discuss with the Government of India the development needs of Bhutan. The Government of India agreed to meet the entire expenditure on the construction of all-weather roads in Bhutan and the defence needs of Bhutan, including the training and equipment of the Bhutanese army. Accordingly, among other things, the construction of road from Phuntsholing to Thimpu began, and it was expected that a jeepable road between Phuntsholing and Paro would be completed by middle of 1961.[48] The delegation received India's assistance to the tune of Rs. 150 million for road building activities in Bhutan. Besides, the delegation finalised a deal with the Government of India for an extra annual grant of Rs. 7 lakhs from 1960 onwards, in addition to the regular annual subsidy of Rs. 5 lakhs.[49]

In 1960, the Royal Government of Bhutan imposed a total ban on trade with Tibet. According to Jigmie Dorji, the ban was first imposed "as a defensive measure" as Bhutanese traders in Tibet were systematically subjected to "anti-Bhutanese" propaganda by the Chinese.[50]

In 1960, China must have realised that irreparable schism was being created between her and Bhutan. So, China offered Bhutan unlimited and unconditional help through unofficial sources. The King of Bhutan rejected the Chinese offer and arrived in New Delhi in February 1961 to discuss Bhutanese-Indian relations in general and Bhutan's economic and defence needs in particular.[51]

The Government of Bhutan inaugurated its development programme and established its Development Department on July 1, 1961. The First Five Year Plan was prepared on behalf of the Government of Bhutan by the Planning Commission of India and entirely financed from grants made by the Government of India. In the same year, the training of the Royal Bhutan Army was formally entrusted to the Indian Army, thereby, by implication at least, bringing Bhutan within the Indian security and defence system.[52]

The next year, on 22nd October 1962, China invaded Tawang in Arunachal and moved forward in the Indian territory till unilateral declaration of ceasefire by China on November 21. During this period. Jigmie Dorji was sent to Delhi for probing the possibilities of Bhutan's admission to the U.N.O. "When Jigmie raised the issue, however, the Foreign Secretary to the Government of India deftly parried by branching out upon rather less sensitive subjects such as the virtues of poultry development in a country like Bhutan whose economy was essentially agricultural."[53]

However, India decided to encourage Bhutan establish gradual contacts with the rest of the world. With India as sponsor, Bhutan first appeared as an observer at the 14th meeting of the Consultative Committee of the Colombo Plan for Co-operative Economic Development in South and South-East Asia held in Melbourne on 19th November 1962.[54] Her admission to United Nations took place much later, on 21st September 1971, on the basis of an application made by the King of Bhutan on 10th December 1970, with India's concurrence in the matter. It may not be a mere coincidence that it was another major period of political crisis in the sub-continent.

The digression apart, Jigmie Dorji's sister, Aji Tashi, who had previously been posted as Governor in eastern Bhutan to effect land settlements, was entrusted to handle all business relating to the Colombo Plan and to lead the Bhutanese delegation at the periodical meetings of that body. In this connection Rustomji wrote:

> There was a mass of statistical data to be furnished to be Colombo Plan Secretariat and Tashi quickly enlisted my services to get into proper shape and to prepare a brochure on Bhutan for the ensuing Colombo Plan meeting at Bangkok. Our difficulty was that statistics on Bhutan were just non-existent. Even the figure of estimated population was no more than a wild guess, and as for detailed break-up of males and females, adults and children, there was nothing we could do but invent. But what was lacking in factual data, was more than made up for by Tashi's dazzling personality.[55]

Rustomji also wrote:

> I was soon to find that most of the activity relating to the launching of Bhutan's Five Year Plan for economic development was centred not around the capital at Thimpu but in the broad, lush adjoining valley of Paro. The reason was not far to seek. The Bhutanese have, by long tradition, been allergic to the outsider. It was obvious that, for some year to come, Bhutan would have no alternative but to induct considerable numbers of outsiders, particularly technicians, for assistance in the processing of her developmental programme. With her traditional suspicion of the foreigner, she might well consider it politic to keep this influx of outsiders at some distance from the heart of the country, symbolized by the capital. Their seclusion in Paro would offer less opportunity to mischievous elements for interference in the country's internal affairs and collection of political intelligence.[56]

However, it is also possible that Paro was chosen with the intention of tactfully bringing it more closely under the central administration. As has been said previously, the Wangchuks did not hold absolute power over Paro region in the past and there was scope for improving upon the existing situation.

Strategies of Development

For the purposes of this paper, the chronological narration may be discontinued at this stage. What is however essential is to note that—

(a) development in Bhutan has been primarily a political decision;

(b) the basic aim of Bhutanese politics is to ensure its status as an independent country and continuance and strengthening of hereditary monarchy;

(c) both Bhutan and India share a common perception of problems arising out of Chinese presence and design on the north. Unless Bhutan opens up and pursues a certain type of developmental policy it may be difficult to achieve the aim of Bhutanese politics on a continuing basis, and also to achieve security for Indian territory; and

(d) in the pre-1959 period, Bhutan was concerned about what was happening to its north but did not consider it necessary to respond to India's suggestions. At that time, India was more concerned than Bhutan in estimating the compulsions of geo-politics in this region. In the post-1959 period, Bhutan is more eager to establish links throughout the world to legitimize its aim in politics, but India appears to allow Bhutan develop as much link as necessary so that bigger powers than India do not take advantage of the situation to the detriment of India's own interests.

These basic points have important bearing on the working out of strategies of development for Bhutan as will be evident from a careful examination of whatever data is available for the country.

During the first ten years of planning, road construction and transport occupied the major attention of planners (Table-1). While it is true that for any effective development of resources and market, such a strategy is indispensable, it should be borne in mind that defence needs also dictated the same course. Long before planning in Bhutan was inaugurated, the importance of road construction for defence and political survival has been repeatedly stressed by the Government of India in all its meetings with the Government of Bhutan. The road links to the south also became essential in view of the fact that a large segment of Bhutanese ruling class have been traders. After the routes to Tibet were closed and trade suspended, they needed alternative source for their transactions and thus, development of easy roads to India suited their requirements as well.

Since 1961, foreign relations and development administration became important components of functions of the Government. This necessitated modernisation of the bureaucracy and creation of an educated elite. Also, to implement developmental works sizeable labour was required. For sometime, Bhutan tried to pool as much labour as was possible from internal sources on a voluntary basis in its traditional way. But it soon proved to be insufficient. Even as late as in 1982, non-nationals from 45.6 per cent in public sector, 47.3 per cent in private sector and 96.2 per cent in the casual labour sector.[57] The Government of Bhutan, therefore, becomes concerned about developing its own human resources and, as such, there is considerable emphasis on education in subsequent plans, particularly the second and third.

The influx of a large number of non-nationals in connection with development works has created a number of problems. The Government of Bhutan has to make arrangement for their provisions while in Bhutan and has to import from India commodities required by them (Table 2). While the Government of India has been giving fund to Bhutan for development planning mainly as grants which does not create any problem as such, the imports made for meeting the excess demand caused by the presence of non-nationals have to be paid for thereby worsening the balance of trade situation (Table 4). Their remittances would also in course of time adversely affect the balance of payment of Bhutan. From Third Plan onwards, development of agriculture, animal husbandry and forestry has occupied very important place in allocation of plan fund. This had to be done for increasing the marketable surplus both at home and abroad (Table 3). The development of primary sector is also becoming essential for releasing manpower from it to the other sectors so that over-dependence on non-national labour can be done away with. In Bhutan, the dimension of this problem may be appreciated if it is remembered that over 94 per cent of people are engaged in agriculture and allied activities (Table 5). The development of primary sector is also assuming further importance in view of the rising prices of most of the wage-goods (Table 6).

The big push in plan investment immediately after 1959 is remarkable. The country which was reluctant to receive aid of Rs. 2 to 4 lakhs before 1959 started receiving Rs. 214 lakhs per year between 1961 to 1966, Rs. 400 lakhs per year between 1966 and 1971, Rs. 353 lakhs between 1971 and 1976, and Rs. 1706 lakhs per year between 1976 and 1981 from India as grants for the execution of its developmental plans. And all this in a country which is otherwise inhabited by a population of 12 lakhs in mid-1982.

The dependence on India of Bhutan for developmental plans can be seen from Table 7. The aid from U.N. system and other international agencies is a small component of total resources mobilised. The contribution of internal resources is smaller still and it will remain so unless revenues of the state are increased at a big stride which is unlikely to be achieved in the short run due to the conservative nature of state politics.

What the dependence on India of Bhutan for her development Plans would imply and also what shape and direction such dependence might take is for the future to unfold. A thorough examination of details in this regard is beyond the scope of this paper but a brief overview of the nature of collaborations and gains for each partner is presented here.

During the third and fourth plan periods the Chukha Hydro-power Project was financed by the Government of India outside the plans. Annual energy output is expected to be about 1,944 GWh, including about 900 GWh in firm energy and 1,044 GWh in secondary energy. Under the 1974 project agreement, India agreed to finance the entire project costs on a 60 per cent grant, 40 per cent loan basis. The loan would be repayable over a 15-year period and carry an interest rate of 5 per cent. India agrees to purchase all surplus power at an agreed rate to be reviewed every four years. The formula to work out the rate has been made covering annual operating costs (defined as the interest on project loan, plus operating and maintenance costs) and allowing the Bhutan Government a 10 per cent return on its equity (considered the grant component). Secondary energy is priced at half of firm energy. The World Bank estimated in 1982 that the tariff would work out to Nu 0.13 per unit firm of energy sold and Nu 0.065 per unit above that.

During the fourth plan the work of Penden Cement Factory began. This is by far the largest industrial venture in Bhutan. Full scale commercial operations have begun in 1981. The Plan has a capacity of 100,000 MT per year. Even though there has been no formal agreement regarding cement sales to India, it is understood that all production in excess of Bhutan's domestic needs would be exported to India. The World Bank report states that cement is being sold in three markets—the domestic market, the regulated Indian market (so-called 'levy' sales) and the free Indian market. The domestic ex-factory price is Nu 665/MT, whereas levy sales to India fetch Rs. 650/MT and the free market sales about Rs. 1,100/MT. The amount Bhutan can sell on the free market is negotiated each year. For 1982, the two Governments agreed that about 12 per cent of anticipated production would be sold in the free market. In that year domestic consumption accounted for about 45 per cent of total production. Thus 43 per cent will be the approximate share of 'levy' sales.

The above two are only illustrative of the emerging pattern of future Indo-Bhutan relations as a result of the massive Plans undertaken within such a short period. And this will create problems of its own in the long run to be sorted out by the joint efforts of both the Governments.

Appendix

Table 1

Percentage Outlays for Five Year Plans in Bhutan, 1961—1986.

Sector	*First Plan 1961-66*	*Second Plan 1966-71*	*Third Plan 1971-76*	*Fourth Plan 1976-81*	*Fifth Plan 1981-86*
Agriculture-Animal Husbandry-Forestry	8.2	17.0	23.0	39.1	23.2
Power-Industry-Mines	2.4	5.0	11.7	20.4	10.0
Public Works-Transport	65.7	40.8	19.8	11.6	20.7
Education-Health	11.7	26.0	27.0	17.0	15.6
Headquarters	3.2	4.3	3.4	3.1	21.2
Others	8.8	6.9	14.7	8.8	9.3
Size of Plan Outlay (in Million Nu)	107.2	202.2	475.2	1106.2	3367.8

Source: Worked out from P.P. Karan and Shigeri Iijima, *Bhutan: Development amid Environmental and Cultural Preservation,* (Tokyo, 1987), p. 20.

Table 2

Composition of Estimated Imports from India, 1981-82.

Item		*Percentage of Total Value*
Consumer Goods		
	Food	12.3
	Non-Food	13.8
	Total	26.1
Intermediate Goods		26.7
Capital Goods		30.5
Unclassified		16.7
	Total	100.0

Note: Food items include rice, wheat, sugar, dairy and meat products, salt, edible oils, etc.; Non-food items include fabrics, stationery, yarn, garments and footwear; Intermediate goods include petroleum products, iron and steel pipes, sheets, bottles, coal, etc. Capital Goods include machinery and equipment besides truck and other automobiles, motor vehicle spares, etc.

Source: *World Bank Report No. 4307-BHU*, p. 128.

Table 3

Composition of Estimated Exports to India, 1981-82

Item	*Per cent of Total Value*
Cement	26.6
Oranges	9.6
Sawn Timber	9.0
Potatoes	8.7
Cardamom	6.1
Talcum Powder	6.1
Rosin	4.0
Processed Foods	2.7
Menthol Products	2.7
Miscellaneous	24.5
Total	100.0

Source: *World Bank Report No. 4307-BHU, p.129.*

Table 4

Balance of Trade, Bhutan : 1980-81 / 1984-85 (in Million Nu)

Year	*India*		*Other Countries*	
	Exports	*Imports*	*Exports*	*Imports*
1980-81	130.0	359.9	1.5	34.6
1981-82	166.2	520.6	5.5	65.3
1982-83	157.0	546.5	2.4	100.0
1983-84	157.2	693.9	3.5	129.4
1984-85	173.0	725.0	6.4	100.2

Source: P.P. Karan and Shigeri Iijima, *op.cit.*, p. 136.

Table 5

Estimated Labour Force in Bhutan, 1981-82

Sector	*Number (in thousand)*	*Per cent of Total*
Agriculture	613	94.3
Industry	6	0.9
Trade	9	1.4
Public Service	22	3.4
Total	650	100.00

Source: *World Bank Report No. 4307-BHU*, p. 82.

Table 6

Rise of Consumer Prices 1977-78 to 1981-82

Item	*Average annual rate of increase*
Cereals	11.2
Pulses	9.8
Vegetables	17.1
Fruit	7.9
Spices	8.1
Edible oil	12.3
Milk and Milk Products	13.8
Other Food and Intoxicants	14.2
Fuel and Light	24.6
Clothing and Footwear	7.3
Stationery	11.8
Furniture and Utensils	18.7
Misc. Goods and Services	17.6
Average	13.4

***Source*:** Royal Government of Bhutan, *Fifth Plan-Main Document*, p. 26.

Table 7

Percentage Resource Mobilisation from Various Sources 1961-81.

Plan Period	*India*	*U.N. System and other International Agencies*	*Internal*
First Plan	100	—	—
Second Plan	99	—	1
Third Plan	90	3	7
Fourth Plan	77	18	5

Source: *Bhutan, Country Economic Memorandum, Vol. 1, Main Report* (Planning Commission, Bhutan), 1988, p. 67.

References

1. Leo E. Rose, The Politics of Bhutan, (Ithaca & London, Cornell University Press, 1977), p. 160.
2. *Ibid.*, p. 161.
3. Nari Rustomji, *Bhutan : The Dragon Kingdom in Crisis*, (Delhi, Oxford University Press, 1978), p. 30.
4. Nari Rustomji, *Enchanted Frontiers*, Paperback edition, (Calcutta, Oxford University Press, 1973, First published 1971), pp. 182-83.
5. *Ibid.*, p. 195.
6. *Ibid.*, p. 182.
7. *Ibid.*, p. 195.
8. *Ibid.*, p. 196.
9. *Ibid.*, p. 165.
10. Suparna Sen, "Indo-Bhutan Trade, 1774-1815", in the *Himalayan*

Miscellany, Vol. 2, No. 1., (March 1988).

11. Rustomji, (1973), *op.cit.*, p. 165.
12. Rustomji, (1978), *op.cit.*, p. 53.
13. Rustomji, (1973), *op.cit.*, p. 176.
14. Rustomji, (1978), *op.cit.*, p. 55.
15. P.P. Karan and Shigeri Iijima, *Bhutan : Development Amid Environmental and Cultural Preservation*, (Tokyo, Institute for the Study of Languages and Cultures of Asia and Africa, 1987), p. 135.
16. Rustomji, (1973), *op.cit.*, p. 182.
17. *Ibid.*, pp. 161-62.
18. *Ibid.*, p. 194.
19. *Ibid.*, p. 203.
20. *Ibid.*, p. 180.
21. *Ibid.*, p. 181.
22. *Ibid.*, p. 180.
23. *Ibid.*, p. 192.
24. *Ibid.*, p. 184.
25. *Ibid.*, p. 183.
26. *Ibid.*, p. 194.
27. *Ibid.*, p. 184.
28. *Ibid.*, p. 184.
29. *Ibid.*, p. 177.
30. *Ibid.*, p. 174, 182.
31. *Ibid.*, p. 178, 193.
32. Ram Rahul, *Royal Bhutan*, (New Delhi, ABC/Publishing House, 1983), p. 32.
33. Suparna Sen and Samar Paul, 'Chinese Invasion of Tibet in 1950 - the Indian Reaction' (Unpublished paper, presented at a Departmental Seminar in the Centre for Himalayan Studies on 23rd February, 1983).
34. Rose, *op. cit.*, p. 73.

35. Rustomji, (1973), *op.cit.*, pp. 159-60.

36. *Ibid.*, pp. 163-64.

37. *Ibid.*, p. 181.

38. *Ibid.*, p. 168.

39. *Ibid.*, p. 193.

40. *Ibid.*, p. 231.

41. S.S. Bhattacharyya, 'Planning Strategy in Bhutan' in *The Himalayas : Profiles of Modernisation and Adaptation*, by S.K. Chaube, (New Delhi, Sterling Publishers Private Ltd., 1985), pp. 210-11.

42. Rustomji, (1973), *op.cit.* p. 236.

43. Rose, *op.cit.*, pp. 75-76n.

44. Richen Dolma Taring, *Daughter of Tibet*, Third Reprint, (New Delhi, Allied Publishers Pvt. Ltd., 1983, First published 1970), pp. 246-55.

45. Rahul, *op.cit.*, p. 58.

46. *Ibid.*, p. 38; Rose says the border was closed in 1960, see Rose, *op.cit.*, p. 76n.

47. Rahul, *op.cit.*, p. 61.

48. Rustomji, (1978), *op.cit.*, p. 25

49. Bhattarcharya, *op.cit.*, p. 211.

50. Rose, *op,cit.*, p. 78.

51. *Ibid.*, pp. 79-80, Bhattarcharya *op.cit.*, pp. 211-12; Rahul, *op.cit.*, p. 39.

52. Rose, *op.cit.*, p. 78.

53. Rustomji, (1978), *op.cit.*, p. 27.

54. Rahul, *op.cit.*, p. 39.

55. Rustomji, (1978), *op.cit.*, p. 32.

56. *Ibid.*, p. 31.

57. *Bhutan : Development in a Himalayan Kingdom*, (Document of the World Bank), p. 83.

8

Development Strategy in the Hill Areas of Darjeeling : A Critical Appraisal

SASWATI BISWAS

The hill areas of Darjeeling constitute a unique part of the state of West Bengal. Geographically as well as socially, the area is different from the rest of West Bengal.

The area received special attention from the British administrators and it is through their writings mainly that the area has become known to us. The interest on the area has been aroused in recent times again and more recently the spurt of writings in newspapers and magazines and even in books has been mainly due to the movement launched by the Gorkha National Liberation Front.

The uniqueness of this area itself demands that studies of different aspects of West Bengal should give special attention to the study of the hill areas. The present paper attempts to evaluate the strategy of development adopted for the hill areas of Darjeeling since the Independence and mainly since the Fifth Five Year Plan when a separate approach towards hill development was worked out.

Development and Strategy

The term 'development' has undergone many changes in its implication from the G.N.P. approach to the idea of social development which is very much in vogue now. For the present purpose, the term would be understood following S.R. Mehta[1] who has developed certain indicators of development at the societal, community and individual levels. Some of the broad indicators of development at the societal level could be economic growth, industrialisation, urbanisation, literacy rate, employment status, agricultural development, health, improved means of communication, technological advancement, the development of art and culture, the scientific and rational outlook of people, stable political institutions and the legitimisation of social action appropriate to the need structure of the people. At the community level, development could be visualised in terms of the mobility of individuals or groups in the social hierarchy, the standard living of people, increased employment opportunities, the provision of infrastructure amenities like health centre, market, school, post office, improved roads and paths, the mechanization of farms, the development of basic industries, a decline in crime rates and collective and rational efforts to solve the problems of the community, the possession of material objects by the individual families, the construction of new houses, bus shelters, play grounds, improved means of communication. The development at the individual level would be reflected by a more rational or scientific outlook, attitudes, values and norms conducive to modernization of groups and communities.

A strategy, as is commonly understood, is a detailed plan for reaching a goal. As such, if the goal is development of a certain place and of the people living there the strategy would mean a detailed plan involving the different sectors of the economy for reaching the goal of development. A detailed plan having a long term objective may, of course, be achieved through short term plans which may be phased out over the whole period.

However, agents of development may draw up their plans, there could be little differences regarding the inclusion of the above mentioned indicators in their ultimate goal. What is important is whether conditions prevail where such development may take place.

The Area

The district of Darjeeling about which we are concerned at present, is the northern most district of West Bengal. The hill areas of Darjeeling comprise three hill sub-divisions of Kurseong, Kalimpong and Darjeeling Sadar. It covers an area of 2417 sq. kms. which accounts for 74.24 pc of the total area of the district and 2.72 pc of the state of West Bengal. The population of the hill areas of Darjeeling is 5,07,155 according to the 1981 census and accounts for 52.4 pc of the population of the district and roughly 1 pc of the total population of West Bengal.[2]

Not only owing to its terrain but also due to its geographical position and hill population who would constitute a cultural minority of the state, the district occupies a distinct position in the state. Therefore, development of Darjeeling district and especially that of the hill areas implies the development of a cultural minority as well as the habitat with which they identify themselves.

Ever since its cessation in 1835 to the East India Company by the Maharaja of Sikkim the district remained a non-regulation district. It was an excluded area and a backward tract till 1937. The expenditure for the internal administration of the district was not subject to the vote of legislature. Under the Government of India Act of 1935 the district became a partially excluded area. It would thus be seen that the district has received special treatment all through. At present, however, the special privileges have been abolished, though the administration retains some pecularities.[3]

At the early stages of the Independence following partition, the northern portion of West Bengal became partially isolated form the rest of the state due to the stoppage of the running of trains through erstwhile East Pakistan in 1949 and this affected developmental activities till fresh links were established.

Evolution of Separate Approach towards Hill Development and Problems of Cultural Minorities

The different aspects of the development strategy for the Darjeeling hills will be taken up in another section of the paper. Prior to that it would be relevant to give here a brief idea about the genesis of a separate approach regarding hill development in India. It would also be apt to discuss some common grievances of cultural minorities inhabiting such hilly areas.

It is now generally accepted that the hill areas offer a distinct set of problems to development administrators. During the first three plans it was thought that acceleration of the rate of growth of the economy as a whole would also solve the problems of the backward regions and the people inhabiting them. But the result was not of that nature and the Fourth Plan considered development of backward regions a separate issue.

The Fifth Five Year Plan had a separate chapter on "Backwardness and Special Areas". It noted "the realisation of the growth potentials of the backward areas should be taken up on a priority basis in order to give practical shape to the ideals of egalitarianism and social justice."[5]

The same strain of thought was evident in the following five year plans too where it was understood that development of backward regions should form part of the exercise involved in the development of the nation as a whole.

The states having large hilly areas were made eligible for 'special central assistance' through hill subplans since the Fifth Five Year Plan. In addition to special consideration for the hill sub-plan, the Central Government also took up a few specific Hill Area Development Projects. Broadly speaking, however, the general approach towards hill development was the same as towards the backward districts of the country. Thus hill areas were accepted as backward areas too.

The main instruments for encouraging development of hilly and backward areas were[6]

(i) Undertaking of specific projects;

(ii) Central subsidy of 15 pc on fixed capital with a maximum of Rs. 15 lakhs;

(iii) Transport subsidy (50 pc from rail head to project location);

(iv) Income tax exemption;

(v) Concessional credit from national and state financial institutions;

(vi) Hire-purchase facility for machinery (through National Small Industries Corporation and State Corporation);

(vii) Price preference by state governments;

(viii) Lower rates for electricity;

(ix) Tax exemptions (e.g. sales tax);

(x) Interest free loans for specific purposes to certain categories.

Therefore, the main component of the hill development programmes seems to be financial assistance and tax concessions.

Regarding the people inhabiting the hill areas it is usually found that a majority of them are relatively poor and backward. A study in 1975[7] showed that the per capita income of the hill areas of Darjeeling was Rs. 295 while that of the state was Rs. 335. It is also true that the areas inhabited by cultural minorities are often found to be the poor regions of a nation. Thus, economic and social protection of minorities gets linked with the development of backward regions. According to P.C. Joshi[8] the social situation of backwardness in the hill areas is due to an inter wining of three factors viz. domination by outsiders, lagging behind others in breaking away from growth retarding values and the large demands made on the people by the natural environment. Whether one agrees to this or not, it is true that cultural groups who inhabit the hill areas have become very sensitive in respect of developing their land of identification as well as the development of the members of their society. Living in secluded areas having a distinct topography without much outside contact and experiencing backwardness in different spheres of life, it becomes difficult for the people to believe that people in other parts of the country are also experiencing problems of backwardness. They, therefore, start identifying their backwardness and problems with the cultural group to which they belong and the geographical area which they inhabit.

Talking about development of cultural minorities also means that it must develop at a rate so that it can keep pace with the majority. Antony E. Alcock says, "agricultural, industrial or touristic or a combination of these is for better or worse, for richer or poorer, the motor for their cultural power and the motor upon which will depend their ability to keep pace with the majority, resists the latter's social and economic pressures and survive the challenges and natural economic development."[9] But, minorities are usually found to dominate in the agricultural sector, though, not often, in a profitable manner. They are quite under-represented in others. This gives rise to problems because when the agricultural sector cannot give further employment it becomes difficult for the unemployed to be absorbed in the other sectors. Moreover, with education the members of the minority have become competitors for employment in the other sectors like services and industry. Thus a strategy for the development of a hilly area which has peculiar social and physical features should make it imperative that programmes and agencies of development have cultural, economic and social significance.

Development Strategy in the Hill Areas of Darjeeling

(i) Studies on the problems of development of Darjeeling hill areas

There is a sort of ambivalence regarding the importance given to the problems of the hill areas of Darjeeling. Studies on the economic problems and different aspects of development of West Bengal have, often, not given adequate importance to the problems of the hill areas. A number of writings may be cited here. Neither the "Techno-economic Survey of West Bengal"[10] brought out by the NCAER nor the "Analytical Study of West Bengal"[11] brought out by the Bengal Chamber of Commerce in 1971 had any specific content regarding the problems of the hill areas of West Bengal.

Another work "Problems of Economic and Planning in West Bengal"[12] was brought out by the Centre for Studies in Social Sciences, Calcutta in 1975. This extensive work had nothing specific to say on the hill areas of Darjeeling district.

The report of the State Planning Board (SPB) of West Bengal on the work done by it SPB in 1974-75 had nothing to say regarding the hill areas of Darjeeling. This becomes clearer when we see the goals and priorities of the Fifth Five Year Plan as laid out by the SPB. It says, "during the fifth plan period, steps have to be taken to ensure balanced industrial development throughout the state. In order to achieve this amongst others, steps would have to be taken to set up or expand growth centres....... Besides these growth centres, industrial development has also to take place in and around certain other pockets of backwardness in the state, including the hill areas."[13] But in the 69 page Chapter on 'Industry and Industrial Planning' in the report there is no definite plan for the industrial development of the hill areas besides stray references. This is quite surprising because it was during the Fifth Five Year Plan that hill area development started getting a special place in development planning. The same is true about the other subjects included in the report of the SPB. Most of the writings on the economic problems and development programmes would reveal the same lacuna.

On the other hand, we find that from time to time the government appointed different committees to identify the problems of the hill areas and to undertake studies for their solution. In 1955 Dr. B.C. Roy, the then Chief Minister of West Bengal felt that the problems affecting the hill areas should be studied afresh by the representatives of the hill people of the district and submit a report to the Government. Accordingly, a committee of twelve members was appointed under the chairmanship of the Labour Minister. They were 'to examine the various problems affecting the hill areas of the Darjeeling District."[14]

In 1975, the Calcutta Metropolitan Organisation and the Silliguri Planning Organisation were directed to carry out a techno-economic survey of the hill areas of Darjeeling. This examines in detail the different sectors of the hill economy and identifies those which can be expanded.[15]

At late as 1983 we find the "West Bengal Consultancy Organisation' bringing out a report on 'Industrial Potential, Survey on the District of Darjeeling'. It says, "the present industrial scenario of the district represents a serious imbalance by way of regional as well as structural composition. The geographical contrasts resulting in differences in the infrastructural availability have brought about a situation where the hill economy is predominant in plantation and skill-based industries while the plains belt has in recent times witnessed growth of modern, small and medium industries particularly in the vicinity of Silliguri. The State Government has been seriously concerned at the poor state of affairs of Darjeeling economy."[16] In order to accelerate the pace of industrial development the directorate of cottage and Small Industries of West Bengal decided to start an industrial potential survey of the area.

The fact that the government had to confess to the "poor state of affairs of Darjeeling economy" in 1983 though a Committee to identify problems of the hill areas were set up as far back as 1955 shows that much was left to be done in the sphere of development of Darjeeling hill areas.

(ii) *Programmes of Development: The Pre-Independence Period to the Fourth Five Year Plan*

During the British period emphasis was given on certain areas only for development purposes. The town of Darjeeling grew mainly as a suitable holiday resort and sanitorium for the Europeans. It was also a centre of education for the Europeans, and a number of schools were set up for the purpose.

In addition to the civic services carried out in the area, development revolved around extension of agriculture, growth of plantations like tea, cinchona and cardamom and cultivation of oranges and potatoes. Here it seems worthy to mention that Dash in his Gazetteer of Darjeeling says that oranges were introduced by the Europeans.[17]

The economic activities initiated by the British resulted in a great deal of improvement in the road communication. The opening of railways and construction of ropeways further improved the facilities for the transport of goods.

Dash writes much in praise about 'development' in his gazetteer. He says development "which had been considerable in spite of pioneering difficulties and interruptions due to political disturbances proceeded with more certainty and momentum" that is since 1866.[18] In, fact, this development seems to be little more than the introduction of some crops and their transportation, the benefits from which would accrue to the British rather than to the local people.

The developmental activities pursued in the area after independence was of a general nature, there was no specific approach towards hill development. Whatever information is available applies to the district as a whole.[19] During the First Five Year Plan Community Development Programmes were undertaken and by 1963-64 Darjeeling district was covered by ten Community Development Blocks. The district was divided into ten blocks and agricultural extension officers were posted to look after the implementation of agricultural programmes. Other departments like those of veterinary, livestock, forest, agricultural marketing, cooperative, industry, panchayat etc. worked side by side.

In 1958 Panchayats and Anchal Panchayats were introduced and the Zilla Parishad came into existence in 1964. Till the Third Plan period we do not really find a strategy for the development of the hills. What was going on was the planning out of a number of schemes under certain heads which applied to the plains area too.

During the Fourth Five Year Plan period we find that the government earmarked certain funds for development of hill areas, but there was no well thought out plan of action. The State Government had also set up an Advisory Committee in 1972 to supervise, coordinate and speed up the implementation of developmental schemes in the hill areas.[20] Though this Committee did some work, the hill areas drew serious attention from planners only from the Fifth Five Year Plan. This came alongwith the importance given to the development of backward areas in the rest of the country. Thus it was only in the seventies that a separate approach for hill development received due attention.

(iii) The Fifth Five Year Plan

It was in 1974 that a draft plan for the development of Darjeeling hills was drawn up by the District Office in consultation with the Darjeeling District Planning Committee, the Darjeeling Hill Areas Development Advisory Committee and the final approval of the Planning Commission.[21]

In 1974, the Hill Development Council came up as a statutory body with the Chief Minister as its Chairman. The Minister of State, Hill Affairs and the Minister of State, Forests and Tourism became Vice-Chairman of the Council. The District Magistrate, Darjeeling was its Member-Secretary. The Council was supposed to act as the decision making authority in all matters relating to formulation of policy and in setting of broad guidelines as well as in evaluating the scheme in the field.[22]

However, there was no separate machinery for the implementation of hill development schemes. Each government department drew and executed the schemes falling within its sphere of activity subject to the overall direction and control of the Development and Planning Department.

For performing this function the Development and Planning Department set up the Hill Affairs Branch Secretariat at Darjeeling in 1981.[23] The Branch Secretariat is headed by the Jalpaiguri Divisional Commissioner in his official capacity as Secretary of the Department. It has the District Magistrate and the Additional District Magistrate (Development) as Deputy Secretaries. In addition, there is one Assistant Secretary and other Ministerial staff. Matters relating to engineering works are supervised by an executive engineer.

The functions of the Secretariat are to oversee and coordinate the implementation of the development schemes in the hill areas and help them in formulating programmes under the provisions of the Hill Areas Plan. The Secretariat is also required to monitor and evaluate the progress made in different schemes under the plans. It should be mentioned here that the Secretariat has not yet started the monitoring and evaluation of schemes, for this it is totally dependent on the different government departments. Moreover, the secretariat has power to plan the expenditure only from the central assistance provided for the hills, while development expenditure in the hills is incurred from three sources, (a) state plan (b) hill affairs budget of the state plan (c) central assistance.

We thus have on the one hand the Secretariat at Darjeeling which deals with the central assistance and the state government departments dealing with the state plan, and hill affairs budget of the state plan. What happens is that plans come up from the different departments at the district level and are finalised and ratified by the Branch Secretariat and different departments at the state headquarters according to the amount of money available from different sources.

(iv) Fifth Five Year Plan Outlay and Expenditure

We will now see whether there has really been any change in the planning and implementation of development scheme since the new bodies for hill development started functioning.

During the fifth plan period, major emphasis was laid on the employment generating sectors leading to higher productivity. Apart from agriculture special emphasis was laid on the promotion of subsidiary income generating occupations like horticulture, sericulture, cottage and small scale industries, etc. Emphasis was given on the development of 'target groups' and hill development programmes were linked with those of the Small Farmers, Development Agency (SFDA), Marginal Farmers and Agricultural Labour Agency (MFALA) and Tribal Development Programmes.[24] The total outlay for the period (1974-75 to 1978-79) was Rs. 34.16 crores while the expenditure was Rs. 37.22 crores. The sectoral expenditure for the period 1974-75 to 1978-79 was 45.0 pc in directly productive activities like agriculture, horticulture, animal husbandry, fisheries, forests, minerals, cinchona, sericulture and cottage and small scale industries 33.7 pc in economic infrastructure like transport, irrigations, tourism and community development, 18.5 pc in social and community services like education, water supply, municipal services, medical services, power, scheduled caste, scheduled tribe etc. and 1.8 pc in others.[25]

The Planning Commission during the Fifth Plan period gave importance to the directly productive activities. It was thought that programmes which gave benefits quickly to the local people should be taken up. For most of the schemes having both a grant and loan component, it was felt necessary to link the credit and development plans. The importance given to the target group approach meant that the schemes undertaken would be mainly those for which assistance would be available form the SFDA and MFALA.

Important sectors like transport power, education, minerals, tourism, health, water were not given much importance. The

Planning Commission "appreciated that the hill areas were poorly served by social and community facilities but these were given lower priority."[25] Moreover, the urban areas seem to have been left out, even the target groups of the urban areas were not considered.

(v) ***Sixth Five Year Plan***

During the Sixth Plan period the overall strategy adopted during the Fifth Plan was proposed to be followed and remained practically unchanged. All sectors which were conservation oriented were supposed to remain as priority sectors within the overall framework of the strategy followed for the programme.[27] However during this period i.e. 1980-85 the SFDA and MFALA were no longer functioning, the hill development programmes were instead linked to the Integrated Rural Development Programme (IRDP) which functioned through the District Rural Development Agencies (DRDA). The approved outlay for the Sixth Plan was Rs. 80.15 crores while the expenditure was Rs. 78.84 crores. The sector wise expenditure under different heads was 55.71 pc on directly productive activities, 22.15 pc on infrastructure and 22.14 pc on social and community services. The fact that many important sectors were not given due attention may be seen from the following heads of expenditure.

Quick results were given such importance that minerals which are at present felt to have some potentiality in the area have received very little importance. The annual plan of the hill areas discuss in detail the survey of coal deposits that is going on in the area, but while 2.97 pc of the Fifth Plan budget was spent in cottage and small scale industries only 0.11 pc was spent on mines and minerals.[28]

The draft plan for Darjeeling hill areas 1980-85 also says, 'the objectives were to identify people residing in the hill areas of Darjeeling who were below the poverty line and with the execution of projects for generating employment to increase their income levels and thereby raise them above the poverty line. Secondary emphasis was laid on the development of infrastructure and on the provision of social and community services."[29]

Table 1

Statement showing the percentage of expenditure during the Sixth Year Plan for Darjeeling Hills.

Heads	*PC of expenditure*
Tourism	2.13
Panchayat	2.24
Community Development	1.81
Transport	8.00
Education	4.02
Medical	2.56
Water	5.74
Municipal Services	2.12
SC, ST	1.33
Power	0.27
Town and Country Planning	0.23

Source: Development and Planning Department, Hill Affairs Branch Secretariat, "Development in Darjeeling Hills, A Review", 1986.

The idea of integrating the IRDP with the hill development programme is thus clear because the IRDP too has the same objective of raising above the poverty line those below it through provision of employment opportunities. But the hill areas have not been treated in any special manner regarding the IRDP schemes. Only some schemes specific to the hills have been included. There is no difference with the plains regarding the treatment given to beneficiaries or the amount of subsidy granted. The total number of beneficiaries if any in the hill blocks would be the same as in the plains.

In my study on IRDP in the hill areas[30] I have tried to show that identification of beneficiaries have not always followed the prescribed rule. A large section of those below the poverty line could not be included in the list of beneficiaries as they had not been able to repay their earlier loans. Schemes like wool knitting could not be taken up by the very poor due to lack of training. The loans too were often used by the agencies to help earlier loan defaulters. Moreover, as mentioned earlier these schemes left the target groups in the urban areas untouched. Employment opportunities too did not come up as desired.

Therefore, the target group approach which was so much linked with the SDA and IRDP really could not be of much help to the target groups. What might have happened was that since the required number of beneficiaries were identified and the stipulated amount was spent it was easier to show results. The quick returns which were sought after were thus achieved.

(vi) The Seventh Five Year Plan

Coming to the Seventh Plan we find that the following areas have received special emphasis.[31]

(a) The development of a comprehensive land use plan for the region.

(b) Afforestation in denuded areas.

(c) The undertaking of forestry programmes in a manner which does not harm the ecology of the region.

(d) Greater effort in the fields of soil conservation.

(e) The development of alternative source of energy for the region.

(f) New schemes to promote floriculture.

(g) Projects to improve urban centres in the hills and to develop them on planned lines.

The approved outlay for the Seventh Plan was Rs. 122.98 crores.[32] Percentage wise the expenditure during the annual plan 1985-86 was 52.51 pc on directly productive activities, 13.66 pc on infrastructure and 33.33 pc on community services.[33]

Until the full term of the plan is completed it will not be possible to say how far the expenditure pattern has changed in accordance with the plan. But if the expenditure of 1985-86 is any indication we have the following percentage of expenditure under the heads suppose to be given importance during the year. For clear understanding the percentage of expenditure on these heads during the Sixth Five Year Plan is also furnished below.

Table 2

A comparative statement showing the percentage of expenditure during the Sixth Plan period and Annual Plan 1985-86.

Heads	*Percentage of Expenditure*	
	1980-85	*1985-86*
Irrigation	.3	3.04
Soil Conservation	13.8	7.5
Drinking Water	5.80	6.82
Forest Development	10.63	11.50
Flor and Fauna	0.38	1.31
Municipal Services	2.12	9.39
Renewable Energy Resources	Nil	Nil

Source : Development and Planning Department, Hill Affairs Branch Secretariat : "Development in Darjeeling Hills, A Review", 1986.

From Table 2 it seems that besides municipal services the expenditure under the other heads has not risen much. Expenditure on irrigation and soil conservation fell while that on energy resources was nil.

It seems that the hill development programmes have not as yet involved a long term plan for the hills through which different sectors could have been developed. The Seventh Plan has shifted its priority even though much remains to be done for the target group. A long term plan where the development of different sectors could be coordinated and phased out has not been taken up.

The Silliguri-Jalpaiguri Development Authority and the Durgapur Development Authority have plans covering a twenty year period, the hill areas of Darjeeling could also have such a plan and the programmes could be phased out during the five year plans. In the words of P. Roy, former Additional District Magistrate of Darjeeling, "As there is no monitoring cell, no performance appraisal of the development schemes can be done, though a rough estimate is attempted at the end of a financial year. Again, as the State Plan schemes are finalised at the state headquarters by the various departments and the Central Assistance portion is finalised at the district level the plan is an integrated one only theoretically. In practice the 'Integrated Hill Plan' is but a loose agglomeration of schemes.[34]

Conclusion

A study of the plans and the expenditures incurred reveal that the hill area development programme is not a very well thought out programme for the all round development of the hill areas of Darjeeling.

The Fifth and Sixth Plans emphasised the provision of employment to the target group and the Seventh Plan has been drawn up keeping the basic priorities of food, work and productivity clearly in view, which would be achieved within a framework of safeguards to preserve and protect the hill areas.[35] But there is no detailed plan as to how these would be achieved even when it is well known that similar programmes have very often not been able to realise the desired objectives.

Moreover, as the hill development programmes is being implemented by the already existing agencies and departments, implementation is likely to proceed as it had gone in the earlier years, which has not been very commendable.

A strategy of development would include well thought out plan regarding the important sectors of the economy and the aspects affecting the lives of the people. But this is not found in practice. For instance, there is no separate approach towards solving the problems of health in the hills. In the hills a larger number of health centres than in the plains is necessary due to problems of transport and the nature of the terrain. But no steps have been taken in this regard.

In the field of education too, the number of schools especially primary ones ought to be more than what is found in the plains. But here too, the planners do not have a different policy for the hills.

It is now generally agreed that traditional agriculture is not profitable in the hills due to low productivity. Only 19 pc of the land is cultivable and 14 pc is cultivated.[36] It is suggested that farmers should shift to seed production, floriculture, horticulture, etc. These activities require training and expertise. Unless the farmers (most of whom are small and marginal ones) are convinced that seed production, etc. are profitable they are not likely to shift over. But there is no provision for large scale training, assistance and education. Even crops like HYV maize, paddy, turmeric and ginger are not grown widely by the small and marginal farmers.

Cultivation of cauliflower seeds requires the farmer to forego paddy cultivation for one year. A lot of care is also necessary for growing such seeds and even progressive farmers have incurred losses quite often. Marginal and small farmers can hardly afford to take such chances. Moreover, there are problems of marketing and transport which have not received due attention.

Darjeeling coal which can be mined and where surveys are going on have received little attention. *The Statesman* of 24th August, 1985 wrote "the State Industries Department is eager to reopen the mines because it believes that the smokeless coal it would get out of it would go a long way in meeting the fuel demands of the people in North Bengal ..... Fuel crisis in North Bengal has touched a new high following banning of felling in the Neora Valley. Sources felt that should coal be mined in Darjeeling district and border areas of Jalpaiguri district illegal felling of timber in the forests of North Bengal could be curbed to some extent."[37] The reason for low investment in mines and minerals could be because it would take some time to get returns from them, and the Planning Commission has been encouraging quick return schemes only.

Of the three hill subdivision, only Kalimpong has a considerable portion of land fit for agriculture and allied services. Tea is mainly grown in the other area and is in the hands of private owners. The tea industry is not in a good state now. Productivity per hectare has been less than half of all India levels. Employment has also fallen. In 1951 the industry employed 60,979 persons, in 1971 - 56,900 persons, in 1976 - 44,790 persons and in 1980 - 45,987 persons. Participation of female workers as also declined.[38]

Considering the fact that the tea industry is looked upon as a source of employment by a large section of the hill people, should not a proper strategy of development see to it that the industry thrives so that the labourers too can prosper?

The government planners in charge of hill development has no authority over the tea gardens. It is the Tea Board which lays plans for the development of the tea gardens. But the Tea Board also has not been very consistent and has looked after the interest of the owners mainly.[39] The Draft Seventh Five Year Plan for the hills of Darjeeling 1985-86 to 1989-90 is different from the earlier scheme for reviving the tea industry during the ten year period 1983-1993. The earlier ten year scheme had an outlay of Rs. 43 crore which covered activities like extension of 2,000 hectares, replantation on 4,500 hectares, interplanting on 3,000 hectares and other activities. The Seventh Plan proposed an outlay of Rs. 22.47 crore for the hill areas for development activities such as, extension of area under tea by 250 hectares, replanting on 500 hectares, rejuvenation/ renovation and infilling on 1,500 hectares apart from activities such as irrigation, drainage, new machinery, etc.

Such inconsistencies and the condition of the industry raise the question as to whether it is really possible to develop the hill areas without taking the tea industry into proper consideration. That it not only from the owners angle but that of the local people who derive their source of livelihood from the industry.

The rate of urbanisation in the hill areas has been one of the lowest in the state. The contribution of urban population to the hill area population during the period 1931-71 slumped down from 86 pc to 45 pc. In Silliguri it shot up from 14 pc to 554 pc.[40] Steps taken for urban development have been dropped later on. There has been no follow-up of the "Urban Renewal Programme of Darjeeling Town" carried out by the Silliguri Planning Commission.

The report on "Integrated Urban Development Proposal for Darjeeling and Kalimpong" prepared by the Housing Development Corporations, New Delhi, provides detailed plans and expenditure outlays for urban development, but there has been no follow-up action on it, nor has there been any follow-up of the very extensive "Techno Economic Survey of the Hill Areas of Darjeeling", undertaken in 1975.

From the study it, therefore, seems that development planners have not as yet laid out detailed plans for reaching the goal of development of the hill areas. A strategy of development, it seems, has not been evolved as yet.

Many things are to be done for developing the hills areas of Darjeeling. Matters which demand attention include land utilitsation, multiple cropping, forests, tea gardens, cash crops, animal husbandry, medicinal plants, horticulture, floriculture, sericulture, mineral resources, industry, hydro-electric power, roads, marketing organisation, health, education and employment.

The Techno Economic Survey of 1975 says that programmes regarding the above "must be so organised that they lead to the quickest possible development for economic growth. For the selection of proper priorities from amongst these an essential pre-requisite is a deep understanding of the natural and human resources of the hill areas, their present stage of development, their future potential and the problems involved in the process of their development.... Adhoc selection of programmes may be necessary at times but is certainly not the ideal procedure to follow".[41] The contention that development of areas which have distinct social and physical features should have cultural and social significance has also not been looked into.

References

1. S.R. Mehta—"Planning and Social Theory" in S.L. Sharma ed. *Development, Socio-cultural Dimensions*, (Jaipur, Rawat Publications 1986), pp. 40-42.
2. Govt. of West Bengal, *Integrated Annual Plan for Darjeeling Hill Areas*—1987-88.
3. Govt. of West Bengal, *Report of the Darjeeling Enquiry Committee*, (Calcutta 1961).
4. *Ibid.*
5. Govt. of India, Planning Commission : *Draft Fifth Five Year* 1974-79, Vol. II p. 82.
6. S.K. Goyal—"Policies of Uplift of the Hilly and Backward District in India. A Critique", in *Development of Hill Areas, Issues and Approaches*, ed. by T.S. Papal, (Bombay, Himalaya Publishing House, 1983), p. 60.
7. CMPO and Silliguri Planning Organisation. *A Techno Economic Survey of the Hill Areas in Darjeeling*, (Calcutta, Govt. of West Bengal, 1975), p. xxxviii.
8. P.C. Joshi—"Perspectives of Planners from the Above Peoples' Perceptions from Below. The Problem of Bridging in Hiatus", in T.S. Papala (ed), *op.cit.*, p. 35.

9. Antony E. Alcock, "The Development of Government Attitudes to Cultural Minorities" in *The Future of Cultural Minorities* ed. by Antony E. Alcock et. al. (London, Macmillan Press, 1977), p. 112.

10. NCAER: *A Techno Economic Survey of West Bengal* (Calcutta, 1971).

11. Bengal Chamber of Commerce : *An Analytical Study of West Bengal*, (Calcutta, 1971).

12. A. Sen & N. Bandyopadhyaya, *Problems of the Economy and Planning in West Bengal*, (Calcutta, Centre for Studies in Social Sciences, 1975).

13. Govt. of West Bengal, *Report on the Working of the State Planning Board*, 1974-75.

14. Govt. of West Bengal, *Report of the Darjeeling Enquiry Committee* (Calcutta, 1961).

15. CMPO and Silliguri Planning Organisation, *op.cit.*

16. West Bengal Consultancy Organisation, "A Report on *Industrial Potential Survey of the District of Darjeeling*," (Calcutta, 1983).

17. (a) A.J. Dash, *Bengal District Gazetteers*, (1947), p. 41.

    (b) The name of a locality like 'Chhalumthang' in Kalimpong (Chhalum meaning oranges in the Lepcha language) suggests that oranges were grown even before the British came in. This is because after annexation it was the Nepalese who settled in the area and it is not likely that a Lepcha name would be given to the place.

18. *Ibid.*

19. B. Ray; *District Census Handbook, Darjeeling*, 1961.

20. P. Ray - "Planning for Development of the Hill Areas" in *"The Eastern Himalayas, Environment and Economy"* ed. By R.L. Sarkar and M.P. Lama (Lucknow, Atma Ram and Sons 1986), p. 319.

21. *Ibid.*

22. Govt. of West Bengal: *Development in Darjeeling Hill Areas*, A Review (1986), p. 2.

23. *Ibid.*

24. P. Ray, *op.cit.*, p. 321.

25. *Ibid.*

26. *Ibid.*

27. S. Mitra—"The Accelerated Hill Development Programme, Plans and Strategies' in *Hill Development Programmes, Plans and Strategies* ed. by R.L. Sarkar (Darjeeling, HE. 1983), p. 41.

28. Govt. of West Bengal : *Development of Darjeeling Hills* : A Review (1986).

29. Govt. of West Bengal : *Draft Plan for Darjeeling Hill Areas*, 1980-85.

30. Saswati Biswas, *Impact of Development Agencies on the Eastern Himalayas with specific reference to West Bengal : A Study of Two Villages.* (Unpublished Ph.D. Thesis, University of North Bengal, 1985).

31. Govt. of West Bengal: *Draft Plan for Darjeeling Hill Areas* 1985-90, p. 2.

32. Data regarding the expenditure in the Seventh Plan is available only for the year 1985-86.

33. Govt. of West Bengal : *Integrated Annual Plan for Darjeeling Hill Areas* 1985-86.

34. P. Ray, *op.cit.*, p. 322.

35. Draft Plan—1980-85.

36. CMPO and Silliguri Planning Organisation : *op.cit.*, p. xiv.

37. *The Statesman*, (Calcutta, August 24th, 1985).

38. M.P. Lama - "The Industry and its Impact on Labour in the Darjeeling Hills" in *Tea Plantation Workers in the Eastern Himalayas*, ed. by, R.L. Sarkar and M.P. Lama (Delhi, Atma Ram & Sons, 1986), p. 6.

39. Sharit K. Bhowmik, "Tea : Gift for Private Sector", *EPW*, Vol. xix, No. 28, (July 14, 1984), p. 1070.

40. CMPO and Siliguri Planning Organisation : *op.cit.*, p. xiv.

41. *Ibid.*, p. iv.

9

Hill Villages of Darjeeling : Aspects of Economy, Ecology and Agricultural Modernization

N.C. CHOUDHURY

and

KANCHAN SARKAR

This paper partly reports the findings of a general study of the socio-economic condition of the hill villages of the Darjeeling district initiated by this University a few years ago under a inter-disciplinary action research programme entitled "Eco-development of Mirik-Sukna region in Balason-Mahananda catchment of Darjeeling district." The Survey was conducted in 10 villages located at different altitudes in the Kurseong and Sadar sub-divisions of the Darjeeling district. We shall mainly present here the nature of the agriculture economy of these villages with special reference to their ecological characteristics and would also assess the extent of agricultural modernization that has taken place in these villages. Our special effort would be to find out the causes of inadequate progress made in the agricultural modernization programmes. The conclusions drawn from the study may be aptly applied to other hill villages of the district as they share certain common characteristics in nature of terrain, crops produced and the extent of adoption of agricultural modernization programmes.

The Villages : Ecology and Demography

The ten surveyed villages differ in their altitude, location, area and population. For analytical purposes we have divided these villages into two clusters—low altitude and high altitude villages clusters. The particulars of these villages are given in Table 1.

Except Lepcha Gaon all the villages in the Plungdung cluster are located at higher altitude. But administratively Lepcha Gaon is included in the Plungdung Village Panchayat. Every village settlement is highly dispersed on the hill slopes and often the altitudinal variation among the houses in the same village ranges from 400 feet to 3000 feet. It may also be observed that the villages are mostly east and south facing obviously to receive more sunshine.

These two village clusters seem to be ecologically different form each other. In the Plungdung area large scale deforestation has probably caused an ecological imbalance which has affected the subsistence activity of the people. In the other group heavy landslides locally known as '*Pairo*' coupled with deforestation has also changed the basic economy of the villages. Besides, the villages in the Saureni cluster are better communicated with main roads leading to the plains and a tea garden is located near it which provides occasional employment to the people.

Increase in population causes a pressure on the environment unless the resource base is developed. The ten villages occupy 1269.10 acres of land area with a population of 2450. The average density comes to about two persons per acre. But as expected,

Table 1

Name of the Villages	*Area in acres*	*Population*	*Altitude (in feet)*	*Aspect*
(A) Saureni village cluster				
1. Bungkulung	34.42	321	1800' - 2200'	East faced
2. Sadhu Gaon	38.42	127	3000' - 3500'	"
3. Dhar Gaon	26.39	86	3000' - 4000'	"
4. Khaptawali	115.48	488	3500' - 4500'	"
(B) Plungdung village cluster				
1. Lepcha Gaon	430.37	193	2000' - 3000'	South faced
2. Bhutia Gaon	199.44	399	3000' - 6000'	East faced
3. Gairi Gaon	81.82	177	3000' - 6000'	"
4. Reying Gaon	52.62	122	3000' - 6000'	South faced
5. Bijua Gaon	152.41	288	4000' - 6000'	East faced
6. Balason Gaon	87.73	249	4000' - 6000'	West faced

the density of population in high altitude villages is considerably lower, almost half, than that of the lower altitude villages. Though, in general, in all the villages the density of population in relation to fixed land area of the village is fairly high, the problem is more acute in the lower villages. The ever increasing demand for new house plots, roads and agricultural land has compelled the people to illegally occupy forest and tea garden lands.

In the population structure of these villages it was noted that the proportion of work-force (men and women above 12 years) was very high, about 69 per cent of the total population. In the sex ration, men out numbered women by 100 : 92. Migration is a recurrent phenomenon in the villages of this district. At the time of this survey (1984-85), it was noted 15 per cent of the population were born outside the villages, of which 5 per cent were born in Nepal.

The literacy rate is also fairly high in these villages—55.5 per cent in the Saureni village cluster and 48.5 per cent in the Plungdung village cluster. Of the literate more than 60 per cent have studied above class V, though the number of highly educated persons, graduate and above, is very small. This fact has some relevance with the awareness of the various developmental schemes operating in the area.

The Villages : Economic Profile

Mounting population pressure, growing unemployment and extreme poverty characterize the economy of the two village clusters. With an area of just 1269.10 acres in the hilly terrain the villages are saddled with a population of 2450. The density of population per acre stands at 1.93 which is quite high considering the nature of the poor agricultural development.

The villages do not have any industry, 68.44 per cent of the population in these villages depend wholly on agriculture. Only a small portion of the population are engaged in service, trade and commerce, the use of fertilizer is minimal and irrigation facilities are poor. The cultivators depend on natural springs and rainfall to irrigate their fields.

The cultivation is carried out on terraces built on slopes, some of which are very narrow (6 to 8 feet wide) particularly in the higher altitude villages. An approximate idea of land-use and land-tenure pattern in the two village clusters is given in Tables 2 and 3.

Table 2

Land-use Pattern in the Two Village Clusters

Type of land-use	*Saureni cluster Pop: 1022 Area: 264.71 acres.*	*Plungdung cluster Pop: 1428 Area: 1004.39 acres*	*Total area (in acres)*
Homestead land	14.77 acres	12.67 acres	27.44
Cultivable dry-land (Sukha Kheti)	151.50 "	752.86 "	904.36
Cultivable wet-land (Pani Kheti)	46.58 "	nil	46.58
Land under share cropping	11.22 "	7.00 "	18.22
Orchard	22.61 "	nil	22.61
Uncultivable waste land	18.03 "	231.86 "	249.89
Total	264.71 "	1004.39 "	1269.10

It can be seen from Table 2 that the proportion of dry-land is very high in all the villages. This is particularly so in the high altitude villages, whatever wet-land is available is exclusively located in the lower villages. The uncultivable waste-land is also significantly high in the higher villages.

Table 3

Classification of Households according to the size of Land-holdings

Villages	*No. of house-holds*	*0.5 to 1 acre*	*Above 1 to 3 acres*	*Above 3 to 10 acres*	*Above 10 to 25 acres*
Saureni cluster					
1. Bungkulung	62	36	21	5	—
2. Sadhu Gaon	22	10	8	4	—
3. Dhar Gaon	14	4	8	2	—
4. Khaptawali	83	46	24	18	—
Total	181	96	61	24	
		(53%)	(34%)	(13%)	
Ilungdung cluster					
1. Lepcha Gaon	36	—	1	16	19
2. Bhutia Gaon	74	18	33	22	1
3. Gairi Gaon	26	11	5	10	—
4 Reying Gaon	20	5	6	8	1
5. Bijua Gaon	46	9	16	20	1
6. Balason Gaon	39	18	15	4	2
Total	241	61	76	80	24
		(25.3%)	(31.6%)	(33.2%)	(10%)

Though some households own quite a sizeable areas of land, a large part of this land is uncultivable, particularly in the higher villages. The per capita holding size of cultivable land in both the lower and upper villages vary from 0.22 acres to 4.41 acres except in the Lepcha Gaon in the Plungdung cluster where it is 1.91 acres per person. In general, most of the cultivators are marginal and small farmers; only a few of them may be called medium farmers.

As noted above, the main occupation of the people is agriculture but the percentage of the population engaged in this work varies from village to village. Taking the two villages clusters as reference points the nature of the primary occupation of the adult population appears as in Table 4.

Table 4

Primary Occupation of the Working Population

Occupation	*Saureni cluster*		*Plungdung cluster*	
	Number	*Percentage*	*Number*	*Percentage*
Cultivation	241	34.58	653	66.64
Service	54	7.75	30	8.16
Trade and Commerce	8	1.14	10	1.02
Agri. labourer	54	7.75	29	2.95
Student	100	14.34	174	17.76
Housework	188	26.98	13	1.32
Others	27	3.88	5	0.52
Non-workers	25	3.58	16	1.63
Total	697	100.00	930	100.00

There is quite a difference in the occupational pattern in the two clusters. Owing to the shortage of land, the working population in the lower village are forced to depend less on agriculture; the number of agriculture labourers is also higher here and so also the number of persons (mostly women) who are engaged in housework exclusively. But this table should be read along with Table 5 which shows the nature of supplementary occupation of the villagers in these two clusters who have some kind of secondary occupation.

Table 5

Supplementary Occupation of the Working Population

Occupation	*Saureni cluster*		*Plungdung cluster*	
	Number	*Percentage*	*Number*	*Percentage*
Cultivation	247	71.80	18	3.48
Service	1	0.29	2	0.38
Agri. labourers	78	22.68	374	72.06
Housework	5	1.46	108	20.80
Others	13	3.77	17	3.28
Total	344	100.00	519	100.00

It is evident from Table 5 that a little more than half of the working population has some kind of secondary occupation in which agriculture, either partly and/or agricultural labour takes the prominent part.

Any programme of agricultural modernization is directly linked with the nature of the crops produced in an area. Maize, millet and paddy are the subsistence crops of the area, but paddy is not grown in the high altitude villages obviously due to the lack of irrigation facilities. At these altitudes maize and potato form the principal crops. In the low altitude villages maize, millet, ginger, squash and orange are grown. Cardamom is grown in both the village clusters. Maize is the basic subsistence food occasionally supplemented by rice whenever available. Potato, orange, squash, ginger and cardamom are primarily grown for export to the plains. Millet is used as well as for making beer.

For these marginal and small farmers, family is the basic production unit. Only a small number of cultivators can afford to hire labourers, that too partially, to augment the family labour. However, a system of mutual exchange of labour exists among people. As expected the Plungdung group of villages being more dependent on agriculture, the employment of hired labourers and exchange labour is more widespread than in the Saureni group. Table 6 gives the actual picture of the labour utilization pattern.

Table 6

Labour Utilization (Percentage of Households)

Village cluster	*Family labour*	*Partially hired labour*	*Exchange labour*
Saureni cluster	73.29	15.94	10.78
Plungdung cluster	58.46	21.37	20.19

On a very rough estimate it was found that in the agricultural year 1984-85 about 16 per cent of the total mandays in the Saureni cluster of villages came from hired labour; in the Plungdung cluster it was 21.5 pre cent. This shows that the major part of the agricultural operations was done by family and exchange labour; the chances of getting employment as hired labour were very little in the villages, though the scope was marginally better in the Plungdung cluster of villages.

Besides agriculture, another occupation of the people is animal husbandry. Almost every household has one or more cows or buffalo, the milk of which is sold either to the milk cooperative or to outside milk traders. This provides the family with some much needed cash income. A census of the cattle in the villages was accordingly taken at the time of the survey, which is given in Table 7.

Table 7

Cattle Census in Relation to Uncultivable Wasteland

Village cluster	*No. of households*	*No. of cattle*	*Uncultivable wasteland (acres)*	*Cattle per acres*
Saureni	181	1141	18.03	63.28
Plungdung	241	1792	231.86	7.73

It is obvious that with so little of waste land available it is not possible to support such a large cattle population. The pressure is more acute in the Saureni group of villages where, theoretically 63 heads of cattle must be supported on one acre of wasteland. The people are, therefore, compelled to go to the nearby forest to collect grass and leaves or send their cattle for grazing to the forest. This over grazing or over exploitation of forest resources is causing unbridled destruction of this natural wealth on the one hand and increasing the misery of the people on the other as the villagers are to cover more and more distance to collect grass, leaves and timber with the shrinking of the forest line. Leaving other ecological depredations apart, this itself is a matter of great concern.

To get an overall picture of the economic situation of the villages an attempt was made to find out the ratio of dependent population to working population. This is represented in Table 8.

Table 8

Index of Dependent Population to Working Population

Villages	*Working population*	*Dependent population*	*Depending index*
Saureni cluster			
1. Bungkulung	127	194	1.52
2. Sadhu Gaon	46	81	1.76
3. Dhar Gaon	39	47	1.20
4. Khaptawali	176	312	1.77
Plungdung cluster			
1. Lepcha Gaon	108	85	0.78
2. Bhutia Gaon	245	154	0.2
3. Gairi Gaon	108	69	0.63
4. Reying Gaon	71	51	0.71
5. Bijua Gaon	154	134	0.87
6. Balason Gaon	132	117	0.88
Total	1206	1244	10.32

Though on an average one earner in the family has to support one dependent, in the Soureni cluster of villages he/she has to support more than one person. In individual cases it may be as high as 3 to 4 persons. When dependence ration is unfavourable and the income is meagre the scope for saving is very much restricted. Very few can afford to save after meeting the basic needs.

Agricultural Modernization

In the rural economy of the hill villages agriculture plays a dominant role. It is, therefore, expected that sufficient attention have been given to modernize the technique of production by providing the necessary inputs. In reality, however, this has been quite contrary to expectations. To understand this phenomenon of modernization we shall examine the nature of irrigation facilities available, input of seeds and chemical fertilizer, application of new techniques and use of institutional financing.

(a) Irrigation

It has been noted that there is a substantial difference in the cropping pattern in the two groups of villages. Maize is the common crop in all the villages but paddy is not grown in upper villages, obviously, due to the lack of irrigation facilities. Potato is the major cash crop in the upper villages which is substituted by other cash crops like ginger, squash and orange in the lower altitude villages. Upper villages do not have any wet-land and the lower villages have only about 27 per cent of cultivable land as wet-land. This predominance of dry-land has seriously hindered the adoption multiple-cropping in these regions.

The traditional source of water in these villages is the innumerable hill streams known as *Khola* in the local language (Nepali). Plots near the streams are irrigated with the help of polythene or rubber pipes. But due to the depletion of forest, heavy soil erosion and landslides the courses of these streams are constantly changing and supply of water to fields is becoming erratic and uncertain. In the upper villages though there are some important perennial streams the water is very deep and it requires special engineering effort to draw water to the higher villages. There is no Minor Surface Irrigation Scheme or River Lift Irrigation Scheme operating in any of these villages. As, such, the fields can only produce maize and potato which require less water. Usually maize is sown in March-April, potato in September-November and harvested a few months later.

Some irrigation facilities are, however, available for the low altitude villages, but these are restricted only to those plots which are near to a water source, and it is the owners of these plots who avail of the opportunity with the help of polythene pipe. They hardly allow others whose terraces may be located at a distance, to draw water from the source through pipes drawn across their fields. It has been seen that usually more affluent farmers have their fields located near a water source with the result that the poor and small farmers are often deprived of even this meagre irrigation facility. What is needed is a sound irrigation scheme attuned to the topographical features of the area and its proper implementation.

(b) Technology and Inputs

No use of chemical fertilizer is made in any of the villages except for potato cultivation. Only in one village—Sadhu Gaon in lower altitude, some fertilizer (about 5 kg.) was used in 1984-85 to grow maize. For other crops like paddy, millet, cardamom squash, ginger,cow-dung manure is used as fertilizer. Seeds and technology of production are also traditional. No application of high yielding variety of seeds or improved method of cultivation was noticed in any of the villages.

In the case of potato cultivation, however, all the six villages in the higher altitudes were seen using substantial quantity of chemical fertilizer. All the potato growers used about 50,000 kg. of potato seeds and 9000 kg. of chemical fertilizer in one season. Potato being an important cash crop the farmers do not hesitate to invest in this crop. It requires less water and seems to be suitable for the upland soil.

The selective use of fertilizer goes to prove that the farmers are quite aware of the new inputs and technology but probably due to poor condition of the soil, lack of irrigation facilities and poverty do not consider it worthwhile to apply these inputs in other crops.

(c) Institutional Financing

One yardstick of rural development is the amount of investment made in various productive enterprises. Records of the various institutional agencies and personal interview of the householders reveal that more than 50 per cent of households have taken loans from various sources mostly for the purpose of purchasing milch cattle and investment in cultivation of cash crops. Table 9 gives some idea about the nature and source of these loans.

Table 9

Villages	*Milch cattle*	*Bullock*	*Goat/Pig*	*Cultivation*	*Other purpose*
Saureni cluster					
1. Bungkulung	9	—	3	2	3
2. Sadhu Gaon	6	—	1	4	4
3. Dhar Gaon	6	—	—	1	—
4. Khaptawali	21	1	1	28	4
Plungdung cluster					
1. Lepcha Gaon	20	—	—	1	2
2. Bhutia Gaon	30	—	4	5	—
3. Gairi Gaon	12	—	—	—	—
4. Raying Gaon	6	—	—	9	1
5. Bijua Gaon	23	—	1	3	—
6. Balason Gaon	10	—	—	1	—
Total	143	1	10	54	14

Of the 222 cases of loans reported almost in two-thirds instances of loans have been secured to purchase milch cattle. The number of cases of agricultural loan is relatively small and were taken mostly for potato, ginger and squash cultivation. From

1979 onwards institutional financing has been the main source of loans. All these loans have been taken during the period 1980 to 1985. State Bank of India, Farmers' Cooperative Society and Gramin Bank have given most of the loans, only in sixteen cases the local *mahajans* (Grocers) have given small loans for the purchase of cattle. In four instances relatives and friends have given loans for house building, medical and family expenses. The amount of loan from institutions ranged from Rs. 1500/- to Rs. 4000/- for cattle and cultivation and Rs. 1000/- for raising pigs and goats. In almost all cases these loans were advanced against land mortgage. The loans from *mahajans* and relatives rated much less than that secured from institutions. Three cases of loans under DRDA and SFDA schemes were obtained for the purpose of cow.

Summary and Conclusion

The above description of the economic life of the people in the ten villages studied, bring to light certain features, which we believe are shared by the hill region of this part of the country as a whole. In adopting a strategy for overall rural development of this region these features should be taken into consideration. But in practice, this has not been so as our experience tells. Let us now examine these facts in some detail.

The first and foremost point that should be mentioned is that this region bears some special ecological characteristics. The whole area was once heavily wooded and during the last one hundred years or so human settlements have come up in the hill-slopes and valleys causing gradual depletion of forest resources. As the population pressure increased, migration being one of the causes, more and more forests were cut down and the villages established. With hard labour people built terraces on the slopes and undulating valleys. But even then, very little of land could be made cultivable, which automatically restricted the size of the villages. So we find that the villages on an average contain 40-42 households. The pressure of population has been so great that the people have been forced to occupy government land. In one such instance we noted that in the Soureni village cluster in the valley a stretch of government land measuring about 2000 metres by 100 metres has been illegally settled by people from higher altitude villages. About 10 cattlesheds have been built and the area is used for grazing. Such land is known as *Vashme* or *Baisey* land. Altitudinal differences in the villages have caused variation in the cropping pattern. In high altitude villages paddy is not cultivated, but potato has become the major cash crop here. In the low altitude villages paddy, though grown, other crops like maize, ginger, squash and oranges have taken precedence. On the whole it appears that the people have, without any new inputs, maximized the productive capability of the land. Had there been irrigation facilities and new inputs they could have further diversified the cropping pattern. Absence of Rabi crop in the lower regions is specially noteworthy in this context.

Size of the operational holding of cultivable land being very small, most of the farmers are small or marginal. This has put a severe constraint to agricultural development. For such category of farmers further investment to modernize the agriculture does not seem to be economically viable. What is needed is a different strategy for agricultural development with new crops adapted to the hill conditions followed up by intensive extension service. This could come in the form of agricultural cooperatives and stress on cash crops with proper marketing facilities.

Though schemes like DRDA, SFDA and IRDP programmes have been initiated in these villages since 1970, very few farmers have taken advantage of these schemes for cultivation purpose. Whatever few cases have been reported in these villages the loans were taken for growing ginger, squash and potato and none for any food crop. Absence of use of high yielding variety of seeds for paddy is noteworthy. It is not that the farmers are ignorant about these programmes, most of them are literate and knowledgeable, but they do not consider it worthwhile to go through the process of bureaucratic machinery and visit the block office repeatedly for an uneconomic cause. They have rather gone more for cattle, goat or pig loan from the Banks and Cooperative Society than agricultural loans. Under the prevailing circumstances perhaps, that has been a wiser choice though the presence of a large number of cattle, in the long run, will affect the ecology of the area.

Use of new agricultural technology and inputs like chemical fertilizer though restricted to the growing of cash crops like potato and to some extent ginger and squash goes to prove that the farmers are not ignorant about them, but have used them only wherever they found their use economically profitable. This again goes to show their wisdom in selecting such alternatives which would prove more beneficial and attuned to the environment and reject the others which would not give them any significant relief. Success of rural development programmes to a large extent depends upon promoting the choice of alternative expressed by the recipient group.

While concluding this paper we would like to mention that special agricultural modernization plan suited to the felt needs of the people and the ecology of the region should have been adopted in all these years. In such a plan, irrigation for the dry lands must take a prominent place. This will help diversification of the cropping pattern. New crops, specially suited to the higher altitude villages need to be introduced. The seed farms should be entrusted with this responsibility of experimenting and developing new crops. There is also scope for developing further the present cash crops like potato, ginger, squash and orange. Economic return from cash crops seems to be much more than investment in food crops. People are quite aware of this fact. What they need is the proper encouragement and regular extension service. In substance that we are suggesting is a micro-region comprehensive planning and its proper execution for the region.

But even with scientific management of agriculture and substantial increase in production we feel that agriculture alone cannot solve the economic problems of the region. Limitation of land and the nature of terrain cannot possibly cope with increasing population pressure and unemployment. It is, therefore, necessary to expand the employment base by setting up small industries, encouraging such schemes as self employment, piggery, poultry-farming and bee-keeping on a cooperative basis.

Floriculture has also considerable scope in this region. However, a full discussion of this strategy of development is beyond the scope of this paper. But whatever schemes are adopted must be suited to the needs and economic capability of small and marginal farmers.

Acknowledgement

The original research scheme "Study of the Socio-economic Condition of the Hill Villages of the Darjeeling District" was conducted jointly by Prof. N.C. Choudhury and Prof. S.K. Chaube, ex-Director of the Centre for Himalayan Studies. The team of research assistants included Shri Khemraj Sharma, Shri Thaneswar Bir, Shri Aloke Das and Shri Kanchan Sarkar. Shri Sharma and Shri Bir have since left the team. We acknowledge with thanks the help received from the members of the team in the collection and compilation of the data. However, we alone are responsible for the views expressed in the paper.

10

Problems and Strategies of Development in the Darjeeling Himalaya

P.K. CHAKRAVARTY

The entire Himalayas today are exposed to accelerating changes - environmental, economic, socio-cultural and even political. Over saturated plains cannot accommodate any more population pressure. Obvious alternative is human inroads into the hitherto inaccessible, abandoned tracts despite varied physical constraints. Indiscreet interference of the habitat has caused widespread ecological havocs that are clearly manifested in bare slopes, mass wasting, slope failures and gully erosion, raised streambeds, shifting of river courses and braided channels, drying up and recession of water points and springs, changes in climate and hydrological regime, ugly urban-scopes, etc. The fragile ecosystem has undergone extensive changes through excessive human intervention. Although change is inevitable, and desirable, in the modern dynamic society, particularly when it improves the living condition and standard of the local inhabitants, a methodology of slow, steady but gradual change must be found out which is consistent with the preservation of the unique flora and fauna, spectacular natural beauty and distinctive cultures of the Himalayan belt.

Problems of Development

The environmental pollution and poverty are man-made phenomena that are fast extending over the Darjeeling Himalaya. Ecological degradation is manifested in bare hill slopes and ugly landscapes across the whole range. The impact of man upon the mountain ecosystem has created a state of jeopardy and varied biospheric problems. In places like Kalimpong, Tista Bazar, Darjeeling, Kurseong, Tindharia, the over use and misuse of mountain land causes economic losses far in excess of any gains from development endevours. Eco-stresses in the mountains, due to demographic and technological threats, have unending destructive impact in the plains below. Recurrent floods in the Tista and Balason, the siltation of dams and reservoirs (the Jaldhaka), loss of homesteads and agricultural land (the Ambutea Bustee near Kurseong) are all responsible for irreplaceable human and economic losses. Expansion of tourism and associated activities are having unplanned urban growth leading to loss of aesthetic beauty especially around Darjeeling, Kurseong and Kalimpong towns that can be exemplified through the schematic diagrams I and II.

A serious demographic threat is looming large over the region on a larger scale. Since it became a part of British India in 1935, this Himalayan belt has witnessed an unprecedented growth of population upto the present decade. Never before people were so many who are pushing up the hills (Appendix - I)

The situation is still worse in the towns where there is a

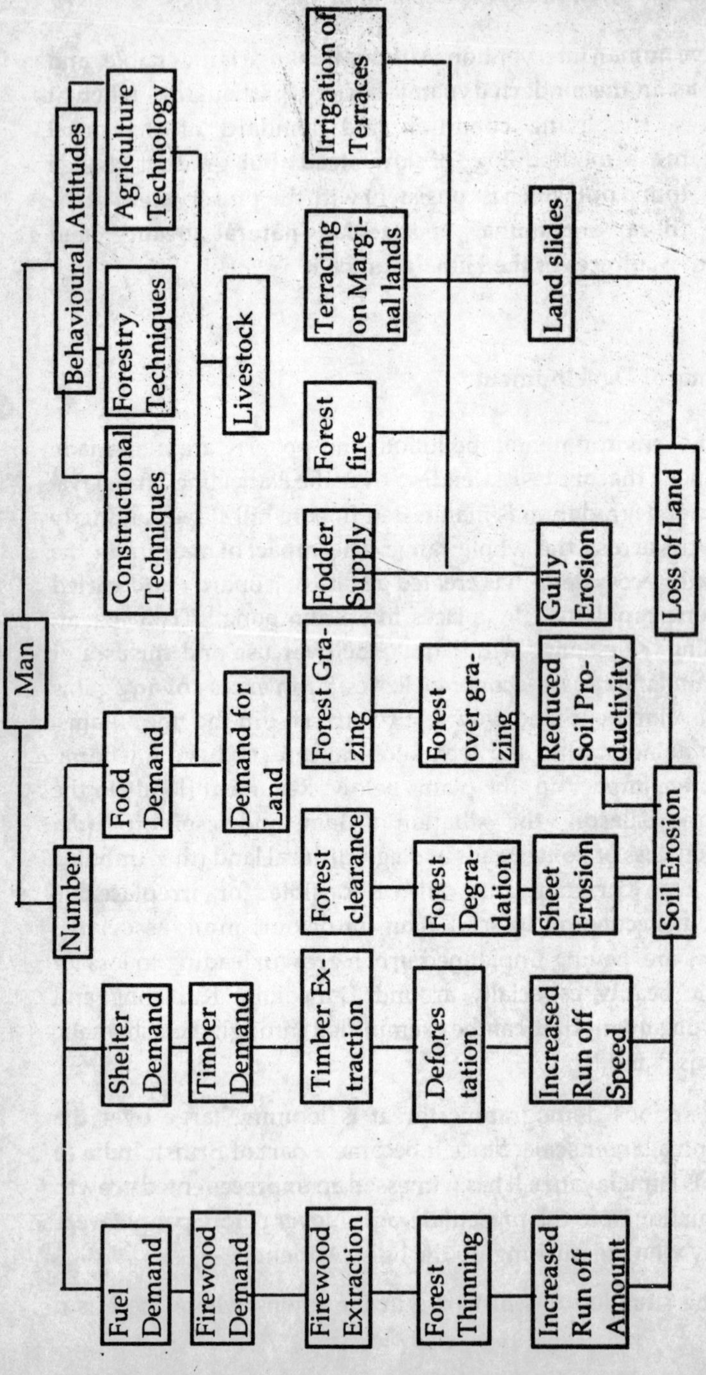

Fig. I

Man made Erosion and Destruction (Modified After Hans C. Reiger

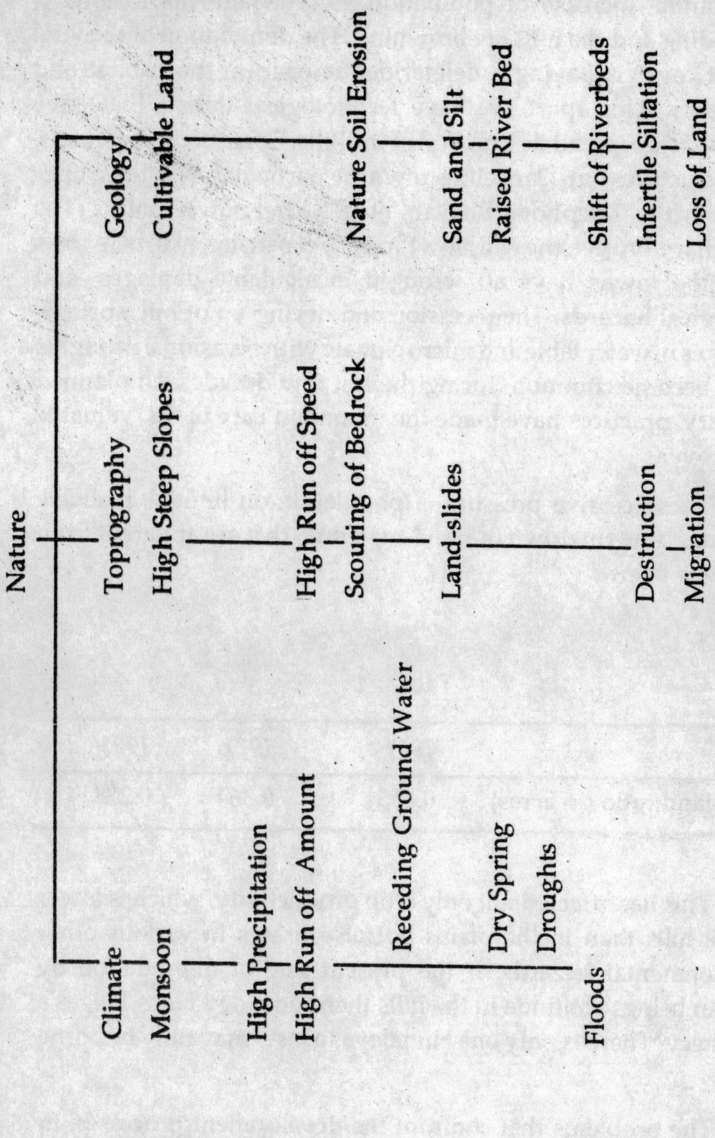

Fig. II

Natural Erosion and Destruction (Modified After Hans. C. Reiger)

substantial increase of population. Everywhere the treeline is receeding and the hills are browning. The denudation of the vital forest cover is having a deleterious impact on the habitat and economy. This apart, we have technological threats that have caused widespread destruction of the hills. Construction of roads, tall structures (at Darjeeling town in particular viz. the Super Market, the Telephone Bhavan, etc.), hydrel power units (The Rammam Project, the Jaldhaka Project), expansion of urban areas near the towns have all wrought incalculable damages and ecological hazards. The recession and drying up of hill springs, changes in water table and micro climate with occasional droughts have become common during the last few decades. Unplanned forestry practices have made the mountain bare of its valuable tree cover.

The excessive pressure of population on limited available land has brought down the land-man ratio that are apparent from the table below:

Table 1

	1961	*1971*	*1981*
Man-land ratio (in acres)	0.455	0.364	0.278

This has affected not only crop productivity, which is lower in the hills than in the plains but also brings in various other environmental hazards. If the present rate of depredation by human beings continue in the hills then some day Hans Reiger's prophecy 'There is only one Himalaya to lose' may fully be borne out.

The problems that confront the development processes, in the Darjeeling Himalaya, are many. Despite a very rich and varied resources base widespread inefficiency among the masses and under development are rampant. Low levels of environmental and socio-economic consciousness and a lack of public awareness about the ecological hazards that are taking place because of excessive human interference, need to be raised through eco-restoration programmes and environmental education. The major constraints to regional economic development are mentioned below :

I. Environmental/Natural Problems

(a) The lie of the land, rugged terrain character, radiating ranges, wide variation in the range of altitude within a short distance (from 200 m to 3600 m), steep slopes are responsible for physical isolation, remoteness and restrained movement (Tonglu, Phalut, Sandakphu, Lava Lolaygaon, Today Tangta areas).

(b) The stratigraphical character, lithology of the area needs special mention. The rock character south of Kurseong are prone to frequent landslides (areas around Rongtong, Chunabhati, Tindharia). This natural erosional processes that occur on a massive scale are difficult to tackle. Moreover, the structural set up due to tectonic instability is prone to various denudational processes.

(c) Natural and man-made erosional agents on the deforested slopes have given rise toseveresoil erosion and associated problems like siltation of river beds, shifting of river courses, gully erosion, mass wasting, landslides, slope failures, braided channels, etc. This perennial problem reduces the top soil cover thus lowering the productive capacity of the soil. Enormous amount of soil from the hills is being lost to the Tista, Rangit, Balason rivers every year and there is no effective means yet evolved to stop the outflow of this vital component of the habitat. Traditional agricultural techniques, removal of forest cover, constructional activities and landslides are responsible for rampant soil erosion.

(d) Hydrological and micro climatic changes are also taking place in the Darjeeling Himalaya because of indiscriminate felling of the tree cover. Fluctuation of ground water table, recession of water points, drying up of springs, occasional droughts, fluctuation of rainfall amount are some of the effects that have been encountered here. Rapid unplanned deforestation is causing loss of valuable endangered species of fauna and change in edaphic condition. Precipitation data, for a period of 25 years, show a change in annual precipitation character.

(e) Depletion of biospheric reserves for timber, fuel wood, extension of cultivation and settlement, fodder for the livestock and uncontrolled grazing have brought about an abrupt change in the ecosystem. Many endangered species of flora and fauna are gradually being vanished and exterminated.

(f) Rapid urban sprawl, road and house building spree are not only eating up forested hill slopes but are creating a detestable ugly landscape, defacement of aesthetic and scenic beauty around the major towns in particular (Darjeeling, Kurseong, Kalimpong, Tindharia, etc.).

(g) Land-man ratio clearly depicts that the percentage of productive land over 2000 m is limited due to climatic severity, edaphic condition, aspect and gradients.

II. Economic Problem

Physical constraints have a direct bearing on the chronic backwardness of the region's economy. The major economic problems are:

(a) Low level of energy and power resources are inadequate for the already existing demand. Further industrialisation and efficient running of the existing establishments are not possible with the existing power output.

(b) Lack of infrastructural facilities (market, capital, transportation, storage and warehousing, etc.) stand as obstacles for further development of the economy.

(c) Lack of trained local manpower on the one hand and dearth of employment opportunities have made the able bodied workers to move out of the hills.

(d) Low land productivity, faulty land use practices, lack of proper soil conservation measures, overstocking of cattle are leading to low agricultural output. Absence of secondary occupation and under employment plague the hardworking labourers.

III. Socio-cultural Problems

Physical handicaps, in the form of terrain character, have obstructed developmental processes. Underdevelopment backwardness are manifested in deep rooted poverty, low level of literacy and ignorance in the rural interiors, lack of trained personnel and infrastructural facilities, conservative outlook, loss of cultural identity through inter-marriage, inter-mixing and modernisation processes that are spreading fast in the Darjeeling Himalaya.

Fortunately, evils of untouchability, caste system and communalism are less pronounced among the hillfolk who live in peace and harmony.

IV. Administrative Problems

The planning policies that are framed need to be implemented with all sincerity. But in reality we find it otherwise. Some of the administrative problems are

(a) Absence of efficient planning machineries.

(b) Bureaucratic and financial constraints.

(c) Poor implementation of the land reform measures.

(d) Absence of strong political will, incoherent and inconsistent system and strategy of development.

(e) General lack of awareness of ecological problems and absence of mass contact program on environmental education.

V. **Special Problems**

(a) A large scale illegal infiltration of Nepalese people from across the western border has occasionally caused socio-political tensions.

(b) Large scale ecological disorders in some sensitive and fragile areas has deteriorated environmental qualities.

(c) Economic frustrations have given rise to a complex political problem.

Objectives and Strategy of Development

Any developmental activity, in the Darjeeling Himalaya, should have the following objectives:

(i) To understand the problems on the optimum utilitsation of the natural and human resources bases and their bearing on the life style and standard of living of the local people.

(ii) To identify constraints and strategic points for new inputs, infrastructures, institutions etc. to stimulate the process of development;

(iii) To assess man-environment ecological relationship and study their changing aspects.

(iv) To devise approaches to educate the people on ecological awareness and involve them in regional development programmes.

In order to achieve the desired effects in the growth of regional income, employment potentials and general improvement in the quality of human life, in this hilly terrain, the following processes should be involved in the formulation of regional development strategies:

(a) Appraisal of resource bases (natural and human) and preparation of resource inventory.

(b) Identification of specific problems in the resource utilisation.

(c) Formulation of action oriented strategies to alleviate the problems and to exploit the full development potential.

(d) Implementation of policy programmes through administrative and social action groups within a time bound framework; and

(e) Evaluation of the effectiveness of the strategies and feeding back the results.

The strategies for development should be channelised on the following lines:

(i) Micro-level integrated resource planning and utilisation of resources (IRDP), decentralisation of growth centres, diversification of economic activities, conservation oriented planning.

(ii) Rural habitat transformation through the creation and improvement of infrastructural facilities (power, transport, education, health and sanitation, credit and marketing facilities, etc.).

(iii) New rural landuse and development policies (new framing techniques in order to check environmental decay) change in cropping pattern, introduction of short duration varieties of crops for higher output/ unit area/unit time, horticulture and vegetable gardening, etc.

(iv) Social and community forestry, scientific forest management, afforestation schemes, finding out alternative sources of energy.

(v) Development of small scale and cottage industries (forest based, tourism based), plantation industries (tea, cinchona), animal based industries.

(vi) Integrated man and biosphere programme.

(vii) Creation of employment potential and local involvement in the planning processes.

(viii) Consideration of catchment area/watershed as an appropriate unit of planning.

(ix) Proper time bound phasing, impact assessment, monitoring and evaluation of the results.

A planned regional development based on the local resource potentials can obviously usher in a new life in the Darjeeling Himalaya.

Appendix I

Decadal Variation in Population of Darjeeling District since 1901

Darjeeling District		*Decadal Variation in Population since 1901*	
Year	*Persons*	*Decade Variation*	*Percentage Decade Variation*
1901	265,780	..	..
1911	279,899	+ 14,119	+ 5.31
1921	294,237	+ 14,339	+ 5.21
1931	332,051	+ 17,824	+ 12.85
1941	390,899	+ 58,838	+ 17.72
1951	459,617	+ 68,718	+ 17.58
1961	624,640	+ 165,623	+ 35.90
1971	781,777	+ 157,137	+ 25.15
1981	1,024,269	+ 242,492	+ 31.01

(*Source*: District Census—Darjeeling 1981).

11

Panchayati Raj Institutions in Sikkim as Instruments of Development

RANJU R. DHAMALA

The introduction of the Panchayati Raj in India is marked by the Government's urge to achieve the twin objectives of democracy and development. It involves three aspects: political, economic and social. Politically, it aims at the development of local leadership to assume responsibilities in the administration of local area development; economically, it is intended to accelerate development process; socially, it tries to develop community sense to strengthen the process of development and spread it over a wider social area.[1]

The present paper attempts to examine the working of Panchayati Raj Institutions in Sikkim in the light of above objectives.

I

Tradition of the Panchayati Raj Institution in Sikkim

Before we start a discussion on the tradition of local government on Sikkim, it is deemed essential to present a brief outline of Sikkim's history, to enable us to understand the working of these institutions in proper perspective.

The history of Sikkim is replete with changes with regard to its political status. According to available records, the first King of Sikkim Phuntshog Namgyal was enthroned in 1642. He was also the first king in the line of Namgyal Dynasty which ruled the country till 1975. Between 1642 and 1861 (Treaty of Tumlong) it was in independent monarchical state. After the signing of the Treaty of Tumlong with the British it became, by all intends, protectorate of the British Government in India. The Chinese recognised the protectorate status of Sikkim under the British at the Chinese Convention 1890.[2] This continued till 1947, and after 1947, even with the withdrawal of the British from the Indian sub-continent, there was no change in its protectorate status but changes in the internal situation was noticeable. During the late 1940's various political parties came into being taking inspiration from the Indian freedom movement. In 1947, they united together to form the Sikkim State Congress. The Party voiced its demand for agrarian and political reforms. On the agrarian front, it demanded for the abolition of landlordism, forced labour and house tax, on the political side, it was in favour of the introduction of representative democracy replacing the prevailing system. To force the palace to concede to its demand, the Sikkim State Congress staged demonstrations and also under took a 'No rent Campaign' asking people not to pay any rent or tax till its demands were met. Despite these, Sikkim continued to be under the monarchy though the king was forced to introduce certain agrarian reforms; a facade of representative system was also introduced with the holding of elections to constitute the

Legislative Assembly as also the constitution of rural local bodies. But the political situation continued to remain fluid till 1973, when the mass uprising against the system and a demand for a large scale reforms rose to a crescendo leading the Government of India to intervene in order to maintain law and order in the state and in 1975, it became the twenty second state of the Indian union.

Introduction of Local Government in Sikkim

Sikkim can claim to the existence of local government to its hoary past. Though in most parts of Sikkim its function consisted of adjudicating quarrels within their area, the institutions of *Zumsha* occupies a special position, not only because they are in existence in the two pockets of Lachen and Lachung in the North Sikkim, but also because they are famed to have existed since a very long period. We find its mention in almost all travelogues of 18th and 19th centuries. J.C. White[3] found it 'very unusual and almost communistic'. Zumsha literally means assembly of people. Till recent past, Zumsha performed socio-judicial functions. It consisted of one president, *Pipon* who was elected for a term of two years by an adult member drawn from each family. The Pipon nominated two *Gyapons* to assist him in the performance of his duties. Besides, there was another assembly consisting of village elders, known as *Gembu* for aiding and advising the *Pipon.* They were also nominated by the Pipon. The Sikkim Panchayat Act 1965 and 1982 allowed this system to continue with slight modification. At present, it consists of two *Pipons,* five *Gambu* (advisors) and two *Chipa* (Accountants). They are elected by the people for a term of one year but they can be re-elected for another term. The two *Gyapons* are nominated by Pipon. The Zumsha does not perform any judicial functions. It undertakes services in the interest of the community, and such other functions as prescribed under the Sikkim Panchayat Act, 1982.

The attempt of the Government to institute statutory local

bodies started form 1948. A brief outline of different experiments in respect of local bodies is given below :

a. *The Panchayat Tribunal, 1948*

The first official attempt to set up panchayati raj institutions in Sikkim was made in 1948. As per the notification of 12th January, 1948,[4] the Panchayat Tribunal, consisting of a landlord and four villagers of that estate, was to be formed. The desire of the palace to constitute Panchayat at Tribunal reflects the political situation during this period. Landlords in Sikkim used to perform two fold functions of judicial and revenue collection within the limits of their estate, but considering the demands voiced by the political parties for agrarian reform, they wanted to be relieved of judicial duties.[5] This had necessitated the formation of Panchayat Tribunal which was empowered to try petty cases of theft, misappropriation, mischief to property and spreading of diseases and fouling of water, etc. However, no Panchayat Tribunal was ever constituted mainly because of the re-organisation of administrative apparatus and constitutions of district offices and courts at the East and West tehsils, after 1949.

b. *The Local Area Panchayat 1951*

Under the Indo-Sikkim Treaty of 1950, both the parties agreed on progressive association of the people with the governance of the state; for that matter in the formation of village panchayat at the local level on an elective basis.[6] Accordingly, Local Area Panchayat came into existence in 1951. The Panchayat as envisaged in the notification was a non-hierarchical body and consisted of five members elected for a term of three years. The *Sarpanch was made responsible for the transaction of business of* the panchayat.

The panchayats were entrusted mainly with welfare functions like establishment of village schools, repair of village paths, etc. It had jurisdiction in civil cases upto a value of Rs. 100/-.[7]

The elections of these bodies were held in the 3rd week of February (between 18th and 26th Feb. 1951) in the East Tehsils and in the West Tehsil these were held between 14th and 20th Feb.

1951. Out of the 52 blocks, elections were held only in 47. Since no safeguard was provided for the indigenous population (reservation of seats for the minority) the National Party called for the boycott of election. It was successful in the North district, where the Bhutia-Lepcha community was dominant.

Though these bodies were elected for a term of three years, no election was held after the expiry of scheduled time and another experiment on self rule came to a naught.

c. *The Sikkim Panchayat Act 1965*

The Sikkim Panchayat Act of 1965 was formulated to consolidate and to amend the laws relating to panchayats in the state with the objectives of good village administration, implementation of developmental programmes ensuring participation of all communities at the village level.[8] For this purpose a non-hierarchical panchayat system with the block panchayat at the village level was introduced.

The block panchayat consisted of five members elected by the villagers who were land revenue payee. The mondal was the ex-officio member having the same rights and duties as any elected members. In order to safeguard the rights of minority it provided that the government would nominate members of the minority community one for each 10% of the minority population of blocks if no member belonging to that community or less than one for every 10% thereof had been elected to the block panchayat. These nominated members too had same rights and discharged same duties as any of elected members. The block panchayat elected president, vice-president and secretary from amongst themselves for a term of three years.

As per the objective of the Act they were to ensure community participation in the implementation of developmental programmes and were also responsible for good village administration. Accordingly a number of welfare, developmental and agency functions were bestowed on them.

The 1965 Act formulated during the reign of Chogyal was

thought by the newly elected government of 1974 as not enough to achieve the true spirit of democratic decentralisation. The system stipulated in the Act, also suffered from many shortcomings and had failed to translate into action its objectives. Hence the Sikkim Panchayat Act, 1982 was enacted which repealed and replaced the 1965 Act.

d. *The Sikkim Panchayat Act ,1982*

The Sikkim Panchayat Act, 1982 was enacted to reorganise the Panchayat with a view to ensuring efficient panchayat administration in the state.

The panchayat system established under this Act differs form the earlier system on many accounts;

(i) stipulates for a two tier panchayat system with gram panchayat at the village level and zilla panchayat at the district level; (ii) the number of members constituting the gram panchayats is raised form five to not more than nine including the nominated members; (iii) provisions is made for the nomination of a scheduled caste or scheduled tribe and one woman member if they are not elected to the body; (iv) the property qualification for both the voter and the candidate stipuiated under the earlier system is removed and the election is conducted on the basis of universal adult suffrage; (v) the scope of function and finance has also been enlarged considerably.

The zilla panchayat consists of all *Sabhapatis* (president) of the gram panchayat within the district, (ex-officio), chairman of municipal corporation (ex-officio) members of the Legislative Assembly elected from the constituencies falling within the district (ex-officio) and a member elected by each Bazar committee under the provisions of Bazar Committee Act, 1969.

II

Function and Working of the Panchayats under the 1965 and 1982 Acts

Under the 1965 Act, the block panchayats were entrusted with welfare, developmental and agency functions. Welfare functions included the construction of public latrines, sanitation, health, hygiene and conservancy; maternity and child welfare; construction, repair and maintenance of school building; taking preventive and remedial measures connected with epidemics, maintenance of burning and burial grounds; recording of births, deaths and marriages; maintenance of civic amenities like water supply, construction of approach road linking each village to the nearest road. The development functions entrusted to the panchayats were development of agriculture, establishment of agriculture farms, grow more food campaign, crop experiment, digging of composit pits, etc., promotion of dairy farms, embankment against flood, minor irrigation, promotion of cottage industry and co-operative.

Besides these, the panchayats were expected to perform those functions referred to it by district officials from time to time.

The 1982 Act makes a distinction between the 'obligatory' and 'other duties' of gram panchayat. Moreover, the scope of functions have been increased considerably. From the long list of function provided in the Act, it is seen that the emphasis has been laid on the welfare functions, such as to provide for sanitation; prevention of public nuisance; creative and preventive measures in respect of any infectious disease; supply of drinking water and the ciearing and disinfecting the sources of water, supply and storage of water; maintenance, repair, construction of village roads and protection thereof; the management of common grazing grounds burning places and public graveyard; maintenance of such records relating to cattle census population, crop census,

census of unemployment persons and such other statistics as may be required; assisting Zilla panchayat in preparing development plans for the area. It is also obligatory on them to assist in the development of agriculture, forestry, animal husbandry, poultry, fisheries village and cottage industries and co-operative.

There is also a long list of 'other duties' of gram panchayat. Mention may be made of a few functions to show the nature of work assigned to them. They have to perform such functions as the State Government may assign to it in respect of primary, social, technical and vocational education; rural dispensaries health centres, maternity and child welfare centres; minor irrigation, grow more food,campaign development of animal husbandry, implementation of land reform measures and distribution of government assistance within the limits of the gram panchayat, promotion of plantation; regulation of fair,,melas, etc.

For the first time in Sikkim, we find the formation of zilla panchayat at the district level. The duties prescribed to it do not essentially differ from that of gram panchayat. Their obligatory duties consist of regulation of melas fairs and hats; construction and maintenance of panchayat ghar, dharmasala and rest house; construction and maintenance of such small irrigation projects as may be specified by the Government and regulation of supply of water for irrigation and drinking purposes; development of land vested in it by the Government, promotion of plantation programmes, social forestry and environmental conservation; establishment and maintenance of primary schools and adult education centres; preparation of plan for the all round development of district with the prior approval of the Government and to coordinate and integrate the development plans and schemes prepared by the gram panchayat within its jurisdiction.

The 'other duties' consist mainly of social services like organisation and maintenance of clubs, library, destitute home; prevention of burglary, etc. as also promotion of agriculture and allied activities connected with it.

Finance

Under the 1965 Act, the sources of finance of block panchayats were (1) entire local rate (house tax @ Rs. 1/- per house), (2) 10% of the total revenue of the block (3) a matching grant by the government for an original work for which public contribution had been collected (4) sanitation and watercess where such services were provided by the block panchayat to the public from its resources.

Under the 1982 Act, the tax base of both gram panchayats and zilla panchayats has been enlarged and are empowered to impose tax on the following amenities or services provided by them, such as, fairs, melas and other entertainments; sanitation, drainage system supply of water for the purpose of drinking or irrigation within the limits of their jurisdiction; grazing lands for grazing animals; on persons for selling goods at the market place; registration of animals sold at the market, use of Dharmasala, etc., slaughter house, and a temporary tax for special works of public utility.

Working of the Panchayats : 1965 and 1982

(a) 1965

The block panchayats constituted under the 1965 Act continued till 1981 and during this period four elections to the block panchayats were held viz. in 1966, 1969, 1972, and 1976.

Under the 1965 Act, the block panchayats were entrusted with welfare and agency functions but in practice, they functioned more like a government agency. During the early period of its formation, people organised themselves through panchayats in meeting their basic needs of water supply, small log or cane bridges, school and playground.[9] 'Grow more food campaign received an added impetus and it was reported that villagers had succeeded in producing two crops in a year. The villagers could widen the acreage under cultivation and improve the production of vegetables, besides the cultivation of cash crops like cardamom, paddy and orange.[10] There was a growing realisation on the part of the government to involve the panchayat leaders in the planning process. Accordingly, presidents of block panchayat participated in the District Planning Committee to help in the formulation of plans. However, this practice was soon discontinued.

This author's study on the Panchayat Raj Institution in Sikkim[11] conducted in 79-81 presented a very dismal picture of these institutions. The block panchayats functioned primarily as the quarrel adjudicating body. Their role in the development was confined to placing of demands to the Government in respect of their area. Their main emphasis while making such demands were on providing drinking water, village road and bridges and minor irrigation. However, they were not directly involved in the implementation of schemes.

After 1974, the panchayats were placed administratively on the Panchayat and Rural Development Department, presently, known as the Rural Development Department. The Department which was responsible for the rural development in Sikkim, formulated the schemes on the basis of demands placed by the different block panchayats, local need and the economic and technical viability. At the implementation stage, the role of panchayats was limited to the selection of contractor for minor schemes whose estimated cost did not exceed Rs. 50,000 and issuing of completion certificate; major schemes were undertaken by the Department. The panchayat's role was thus, evident only at the stage of articulation of demand and nomination of contractor, the direct participation of panchayat or the community at large was minimum.

One of the main reasons for the inability of panchayats to evoke direct participation in developmental process was the paucity of fund. The Act provided that the panchayat fund would consist of entire local rate, 10% of total land revenue matching grant by the government and sanitation and watercess from the services provided by the panchayat to the public, but in practice, they totally depended on their share of land revenue and house tax. The average income from these sources did not come to more than Rs. 200/- per panchayat per annum. They spent the amount mostly on buying stationaries.

Under such conditions, it is too much to expect that panchayats would play any effective role in the developmental process.

(b) 1982

(i) Working of Gram Panchayat

The first election to the gram panchayat was held in January 1983 and the second one in March 1988.

The introduction of two tier panchayats was necessitated by the desire of the Government to overcome the shortcoming of the earlier panchayat system. The functions undertaken by the gram panchayats are maintenance of water supply schemes, maintenance of village road, small bridge, maintenance and repair of minor irrigation channels, mobilising people for tree plantation in the area and selection of beneficiaries for various centres sponsored programmes under IRDP and JRY. For schemes like construction of school building, drinking water supply, irrigation channel and so on, the panchayat acts as an effective body for identifying the schemes needed for their area and place the demand to the Rural Development Department. Once a scheme is sanctioned the work whose estimated amount does not exceed Rs. 5.00 lakhs is awarded to a nominee which has been jointly recommended by the concerned panchayat and the M.L.A. of the area.[12] Finally, the panchayat has to give completion certificate. It is the duty of the panchayat to maintain and repair these amenities (schemes).

Under the Act, panchayats enjoy power of taxation within the limits of its jurisdiction but in practice, no panchayat imposes any tax except a nominal water tax by a few panchayats e.g. Tashiding in the west district.

There is no uniformity of opinion regarding the panchayat's power of taxation. The question was discussed at different State level and District level panchayat sammelans. One of the resolutions adopted at the Panchayat sammelan, 1985[18] stated that the government should fix the rate of taxation to enable the gram panchayats to impose taxes. However, in another such sammelan of 1986, the participants expressed the view that they could not impose any tax for the fear of antagonising the people and that the taxation power should be invested in the government. So far, they are dependent on the government grant alone. Unfortunately, however, no specific formula has been formulated as to the distribution of grants-in-aid. Soon after its formation each gram panchayat was given R. 1000/-. In 1984-85 and 1985-86 the quantum was raised to Rs. 2000/- per annum per panchayat and from 1986-87 Rs. 10,000/- is being given to each panchayat annually irrespective of its size.

For the utilisation of Rs. 10,000/- guidelines were issued by the Secretary of the Rural Development Department which noted: "the panchayat will first decide in their monthly meeting, attended by all panchayat members and if possible with the District Development Officer (DDO) or the panchayat inspector for the utilisation of the panchayat fund. If any work is to be taken up, the technical personnel of the district will prepare the plan and estimate and get it cleared by the panchayat and submit to the DDO and only on his approval the scheme can be implemented and this money utilised."

The letter further maintained that (i) the DDOs were responsible for the audit of the accounts and that (ii) there was no certainty of releasing such fund in future.

The panchayats have not taken up any new schemes on their own. Their expenditure pattern showed that the money was mostly spent on the maintenance and repair of already existing schemes. Besides these, some of the panchayats have constructed school play grounds.

Section 78 of the Act provided 'the accounts of the fund of the gram panchayat or zilla panchayat shall be examined and audited by an auditor appointed in that behalf by the State Government at such time and place and in such manner as the State Government prescribes'. But in practice, the account is audited by the Panchayat

Inspector either on his visit to the area or the reports of accounts are submitted at the office of the DDO. This is again checked and cleared by the DDO.

(ii) Working of Zilla Panchayats

There are four zilla panchayats corresponding to the four districts of the State known as the North, South, East and West District Zilla Panchayats. They were constituted for the first time in April, 1991 and consist of all the gram panchayat presidents of the district and the MLAs of the area.

The *Adhyakshya* and *Upadhyakshya* are elected from among these presidents. In 1991, elections were held in the East, South and West District Zilla Panchayats, but in the North, they were returned unopposed. The district Collector is the *Sachiva* of this body.

The formation of the Zilla Panchayat in 1991 is a novel experience in Sikkim but due to its short tenure of existence, it is difficult to assess their work correctly. Nevertheless, attempt has been made to present an outline of their working during the first one year.

The Zilla Panchayat is responsible for the formulation, coordination and implementation of plan at the district level. It also undertakes a number of welfare and social service functions. The Zilla Panchayat fund consists of income from taxation and government grant. At present, it does not impose any taxes but depends exclusively on the government grant. During 1991-92, out of a total grant of Rs. 9.3 lakh to the South District Zilla Panchayat Rs. 6.47 lakh was earmarked for the implementation of various schemes; The North District Zilla Panchayat received Rs. 7.31 lakh out of which the share of developmental schemes was Rs. 4.56 lakh and in the East District Zilla Panchayat 14.55 lakh was spent on the developmental schemes.[14]

Various plans and projects pertaining to the District is decided at the meeting of Zilla Panchayat attended by the members of Zilla Panchayat, M.L.A.s from whole of the district and the Head of departments at the district, under the Chairmanship of Adhyakshya.

The implementation of schemes, once approved at the meeting is carried out by the organisational set up of respective departments, as the Zilla Panchayat does not have any technical or non-technical staff under it.

However, it must be remembered that not all the programmes of departments need the approval of the Zilla Panchayat. Only a few schemes are transferred to it alongwith a grant by different departments. Zilla Panchayat mainly implements the schemes of the gram panchayats out of the fund allocated to it with the technical staff of Rural Development Department.

A study of the schemes implemented by them show that the emphasis is primarily on the construction of suspension foot bridge, approach road, providing or repair of potable water supply, construction or repair of ICDS centre, school playground, etc.

An Assessment

The process of democratic seed-drilling in a traditional society like Sikkim with pre-ponderance of primordial loyalties has not been an easy task. The policy formulation and implementation were often influenced by diverse ethnic and political factors. Although now and then, there were attempts to decentralise power, the earlier attempts could not make headway.

Nevertheless, in its march towards modernisation Sikkim adopted some political structures to induce popular participation in administration as well as in developmental process, panchayati raj institution being one of them. The Sikkim Panchayat Act, 1965 introduced a non-hierarchical panchayat, but a study of its operation revealed that it could not achieve its objectives. The failure of these bodies were further manifested in the government's desire to abolish the system and introduce a two-tier panchayat bodies. The main consideration which had influenced the introduction of two-tier system were (i) to ensure a close link between the Government and people through Gram Panchayat and Zilla Panchayat, (ii) to bring the Panchayat system at par with the rest of the country consequential to the recommendations by the Ashoka Mehta Committee.

In order to re-organise the panchayats with a view to ensuring efficient panchayat administration in the state, a long list of functions and taxes to be imposed by the panchayats has been provided under the 1982 Act. But in practice, their functions and finance has remained as weak as before. There is no tangible change in the pattern of functioning. The gram panchayats role in the development process has remained confined to the placing of demands and nominating the contractor for implementing the sanctioned schemes.

Notwithstanding these, it can be said that the present bodies have been able to undertake certain functions as per their needs in respect of clearing of village roads and construction and repair of small log bridge, repair of water supply lines, because of the enhanced government grants. It also goes to the credit of these panchayats that not a case of misappropriation or misconduct has been reported nor have they been superseded. In a limited scale, they are performing their duties.

In order to strengthen its role in development, Zilla Panchayat should be more active. At present, the formulation of plans by the Zilla Panchayat for different sectors is more a ritual than a serious and meaningful exercise. It is expected that slowly the function of integrating, coordinating the plans of gram panchayat would be overtaken by the Zilla Panchayat, to ensure a sense of popular participation.

Effective local development requires considerable financial power backed by grants-in-aid. The 1982 Act provides for many sources of revenue but in practice, all these remain untapped. The state should encourage both the Gram Panchayat and Zilla Panchayats to mobilise local resources through taxation to meet the basic needs of their area

The above discussion has shown that the panchayati raj

institutions in Sikkim are yet to achieve the twin objectives of democracy and development. Rural development till now has remained an official programme with a small degree of local participation. It is necessary that the state government should take steps to strengthen Gram Panchayats and Zilla Panchayats so that they could effectively shoulder responsibilities of rural development

This is a revised version of the paper presented at the national seminar on 'Problems and Strategies of Development in the Eastern Himalayas' at the Centre for Himalayan Studies, University of North Bengal

References

1. V.C. Nandedkar, *Local Government Its Role in Development Administration*, Delhi, 1979, p. 183.
2. Convention between Great Britain and China relating to Sikkim and Tibet, 1890, Article 2 Vide L.B. Basnet, *Sikkim A Short Political History*, New Delhi, S. Chand & Co. (Pvt. Ltd.) 1974.
3. J.C. White, Sikkim and Bhutan : *Twenty one year on North East Frontier, 1887-1908* (Indian edition), New Delhi, 1971, p. 79.
4. Office of the Private Secretary to His Highness, the Maharaja of Sikkim (Judicial Branch). Notification No. 3054-254/P.S. 12.1.1948.
5. *Ibid.*
6. Sikkim Darbar Gazetteer Extraordinary, March 23, 1953.
7. Sikkim Darbar Gazette Vol. 1, No. 3, 15.8.51. *Local Area Panchayats in Sikkim, Notification.* Clause 8 (a,b,c,d) Gangtok, 4.8.51.
8. The Sikkim Panchayat Act, 1965.
9. Sikkim Herald, 12 : 168, 4.12.1971.
10. Sikkim Herald, 12 : 111, 21.7.1971.
11. Ranju R. Dhamala, *A Study of Local Self Government and Democratic Decentralisation in Sikkim.* (Unpublished Ph.D. thesis) University of North Bengal, 1985.

12. Govt. of Sikkim, Circular No. 32/Home/89, dt. 22.2.89, Home Department Gangtok. Previously, the limit was Rs. 2.50 lakhs (Memo No. 420/Home/86, dt. 19.2.86.)

13. Panchayat Sammelan 4-5 January, 1985, Resolution No. 2.

14. The figures have been collected from the offices of the Zilla Panchayat, Namchi, Mangan and Gangtok.

INDEX